STITCHES
IN
TIME

STITCHES IN TIME

SUE BRADLEY

BLANDFORD

A BLANDFORD BOOK

First published in the UK
1991 by Blandford
(a Cassell imprint)
Villiers House
41/47 Strand
LONDON
WC2N 5JE

Distributed in the United States
by Sterling Publishing Co., Inc.
387 Park Avenue South, New York, NY 10016-8810

Distributed in Australia
by Capricorn Link (Australia) Pty Ltd
P.O. Box 665, Lane Cove, NSW 2066

British Library Cataloguing in Publication Data

Bradley, Sue
  Stitches in time
  1. Knitting
  746.432

  ISBN 0-7137-2277-0

Printed and bound in Singapore

To my parents for all their lovely work and to Andy for always being there.

Editor:	Louisa McDonnell
Designer:	Clare Finlaison
Artwork:	Barry Walsh
Photography:	Stanli Opperman
Picture research:	Helena Beaufoy
Pattern checkers:	Janet Bentley and
	Marilyn Wilson
Knitters:	Mary Colbeck
	Barbara Davis
	John and Rosemary Heath
	Valerie Ruddle
	Angela Woodhouse
Mannequins:	Adel Rootstein Display
	Mannequins Ltd

Introductions photograph acknowledgements
Academy Editions, London, p131; Ancient Art
and Architecture Collection, London, p9;
Bridgeman Art Library, London, p45; reproduced
by permission of Broadlands, Romsey,
Hampshire, UK, p79; Mary Evans Picture
Library, London, pp119 and 131; Michael
Holford, London, p27; Leeds City Art Galleries,
UK, p145; National Portrait Gallery, London,
p61; *L'Officiel,* Paris, p144; from *Victorian
Fashions & Costumes from Harper's Bazar 1867–
1898* edited by Stella Blum, published Dover
Publications Inc., New York, p118; The Wallace
Collection, London, p99.

Every effort has been made to contact copyright-
holders. It is hoped that any omission will
be excused.

Introductions drawings: Clare Finlaison

CONTENTS

INTRODUCTION

My career as a designer began with a degree in fashion, learning how to design garment shapes and to cut patterns, how to predict looks and to produce commercial collections – but all this wasn't enough. It seemed impossible to find exactly the right type of fabric in terms of colour, pattern and texture to complement my designs, so it made sense to design the fabrics myself. I began by printing on to cloth, which was a good way to create colour and pattern, but lacked texture.

It followed that knitting was the perfect solution. Yarns can be used like paint, with different colours and textures mixed together to create rich and exciting fabrics. At first I was fascinated by the idea that the most intricate knitted garment could be made from a series of knots and lengths of yarn forming thousands of stitches and rows. I began by knitting pictures and trying to develop some of my earlier print ideas, translating the flat pattern into texture. (I laugh now when I look at some of my first

Yarns and sources of inspiration.

samples, especially the wrong side – a terrible mess of loops and ends. Some are quite interesting, because at that stage I had no preconceived ideas about knitting techniques and so did not feel there were any rules to follow!)

However, my development as a knitwear designer began seriously in 1980 when I went to the Royal College of Art in London to study knitted textiles. This gave me the opportunity of spending two years experimenting with yarns and stitches, using as many different techniques as possible to achieve the effects and fabrics I was looking for.

It was during this time that I started to use visual research in order to develop ideas. I needed to free myself from the restrictions of my background in fashion design which had trained me to work closely to a brief designing garments in ready-made fabrics. I wanted to specialize in developing my own fabrics and this led me into researching subjects purely for their decorative value and collecting ideas together in sketchbooks. I would set myself small projects to research and then develop a theme, without necessarily having a particular finished product in mind.

One of my first sources of inspiration was African body painting, masks and jewellery. Using their very strong colours and designs as a basis for Fair Isle patterns, I made a large picture sweater and also translated some African motifs directly into knitted jewellery. Other favourite sources were the glowing icons and enamel work of Byzantium – the combination of rich colours, textures, patterns and imagery, precious stones and metal is endlessly intriguing. Historical costume has also been a strong influence, especially that of the Tudor period; Holbein's portraits in particular have provided wonderful reference material.

My early designs were highly decorative and theatrical creations which were time-consuming to make, and I soon realised that however great the demand there could be no way of earning a living from designing, making and selling one-off garments that took several weeks to complete. So I began to design garments that were easier to produce and could be knitted by other people. For commercial collections, I had to learn to design easy-to-make, reasonably priced knitwear for a specific market, which was at the same time exciting and interesting – quite a lot to ask! It took several collections to build up a reliable clientele of buyers and specialist shops, and to acquire a group of experienced hand-knitters who could produce work of a high standard.

Visual stimuli are still very important to me – I find sources of inspiration everywhere and sometimes combine several completely different ideas in one design. As I work on my commercial collections I am learning all the time and, happily, the business is thriving too; we now sell to shops all over England and America and have started to do business in Australia.

This is how I make a living and I enjoy it, but I feel that my design trademark is the decorative quality of my work. That is where my heart is. This book has enabled me to develop some of the fabric ideas and inspirations which are so important to me.

Stitches in Time is a collection of knitted garments based on historical dress from Ancient Egypt to the 1940s. In it I have tried to reflect some of the images from each historical period as they appear to me; not necessarily to mimic the precise costume details, but to capture the spirit of an era.

For example, the Egyptian Sweater has hardly any direct reference to the garment shapes of Ancient Egypt, but takes hieroglyphic symbols and uses them purely as decoration, while the patterning on the Egyptian Cardigan echoes the colouring and design of the jewellery of the period. The Cavalier Jacket and the 18th-Century Jacket are more costume-inspired and imitate the popular styles of the times.

Sometimes styles are exaggerated as in the bold Byzantine Sweater. This is one of my favourites; I have a passion for decoration, especially jewels and beads, and I love the vivid colours. Another favourite is

the delicate Renaissance Sweater decorated with pearls and net; it has a romantic feeling and yet can be completely transformed into a daytime sweater by working in plain wool or cotton.

At work in my studio.

One of the attractions of these garments is that each one has two variations and can be worked in a variety of yarns or colours with or without the decoration. The main version of each garment is illustrated by a photograph and my own drawings illustrate Versions 2 and 3. There are clear step-by-step diagrams which explain the making-up process, and, to help you choose which sweater to knit, each pattern is graded with one to four symbols to indicate whether the pattern is easy, or suitable for more experienced knitters. The key to the symbols is given under Pattern Notes on page 173.

I wanted each garment to have a character of its own and to be totally individual, independent of seasons or fast-changing fashion trends. These are classic styles and shapes which have a timeless and almost heirloom quality.

Knitting is so creative and versatile and with imagination is easily transformed into a medium which can be highly decorative and patterned, cabled, lacy, slashed open, embroidered, beaded, textured, ribbed, bobbly – there are so many fascinating avenues to explore.

I hope that my ideas will succeed in inspiring you to use your skills to create something exciting and unique.

Happy knitting!

Sue Bradley

ANCIENT EGYPT
INTRODUCTION

Despite its remoteness, Ancient Egypt conjures up vivid pictures in the imagination. However little we may know of the facts and figures of the 3,000 or so recorded years of Ancient Egyptian history (3100-323BC), the name calls to mind images of geometric forms such as the pyramid and obelisk, processions of elegant figures caught in angular movement, and a characteristic palette of colours: turquoise, gold, the yellow of sand, the green of the fertile Nile Valley, and a rich red ochre. Few ancient cultures have made such a strong impression on the modern imagination.

A collar strung with hieroglyphic symbols made from gold, carnelian, turquoise and lapis lazuli. It finishes at each end with a falcon's head, representing the god Horus.

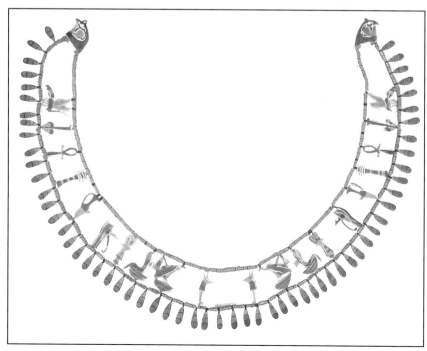

This may be because we have access to a mass of Egyptian artefacts held in museums around the world and displayed in exhibitions such as that of finds from the tomb of the Boy Pharaoh Tutankhamun. But perhaps our interest is also due to a sympathy with the bold visual sense of the artists and craftsmen of Ancient Egypt.

Egyptian art has long been an influence on Western design, and in this century a craze for all things Egyptian was sparked off in 1922 by Howard Carter's much publicized discovery of Tutankhamun's tomb. Unlike most Egyptian royal tombs, long since broken into and plundered, it had been left almost untouched since his burial around 1352BC. In particular, the Art Deco movement of the 1930s took up many Egyptian ideas of both motif and colour. The connection is still evident today. The Egyptian Sweater and Cardigan (see photographs, pages 12 and 22) translate Egyptian style into modern fashion, and, curiously, though the earliest in inspiration of all the designs in this collection, they look among the most up to date.

Both designs show a contrast of ornamentation and severity typical of the Egyptians. They liked to wear magnificent adornments which were made from the metals and semi-precious stones found in abundance in the desert to the south and east – gold, agate, carnelian, chalcedony, feldspar, garnet, jasper, onyx, rock crystal and turquoise – and from imported stones such as lapis lazuli, probably brought from

Afghanistan. The most commonly worn accessory for both men and women was a deep, decorative collar made from strung coloured beads or, in more splendid versions, of gold, enamel and gemstones. They also wore exquisite jewellery, often of striking geometric design: necklaces, diadems, rings, bracelets, armlets, anklets and also amulets – the last important for a people with a powerful regard for the supernatural.

The deep, geometrically-patterned collars of the sweater and cardigan copy the typical Egyptian accessory – far lighter and more comfortable in cotton than the original. On the cardigan the patterning of collar, yokes and sleeves echoes the colours of Egyptian jewellery – gold, turquoise, deep blue and carnelian red – and the cuffs mimic bangles.

In contrast to the magnificence of the jewellery, Egyptian clothing was starkly simple, being usually a length of undyed linen wrapped around the body with the minimum of tailoring. Men wore a loin-cloth held in place by a sash and women wore a rectangle of linen forming a narrow sheath dress supported by shoulder straps which often left the breasts bare. In the more sophisticated period of the New Kingdom both sexes wore long tunics.

Such simplicity of dress was practical. Flax, the raw material from which the linen was made, was one of the main agricultural crops of the Nile Valley and the Egyptians were expert weavers capable of producing cloth nearly as fine as any made today. Then, too, fine, pale-coloured linen, loosely draped, would have been a thankfully cool material to wear in the heat of North Africa and this material is the inspiration for the loose shape and cream-coloured yarn of the sweater and cardigan. Yet the simple style must also have been aesthetically pleasing to those who wore it, a dramatic foil to the splendid colour and patterning of the jewellery – further evidence of the sophisticated Egyptian eye.

The motifs chosen to decorate the sweater are taken not from clothing but from hieroglyphs, the pictorial script seen painted and inscribed on walls and sarcophagi, or written on papyrus manuscripts. Unlike our purely abstract phonetic script, hieroglyphic represents words by images, and some symbols were even taken as magical substitutes for the god, animal or object that they represented – a system of writing that reflected the Egyptian view of the world. Some seven hundred years after the Greek occupation of Egypt in 332BC, the understanding of the hieroglyphs was lost,

and for the next fifteen hundred years the script was unread, a pattern of images that seemed as enigmatic as the Sphinx.

The puzzle came to fascinate scholars, and the key, a slab of black basalt, known as the Rosetta Stone, now in the British Museum, was only discovered in 1799. It is inscribed with a decree in three different scripts: Greek, demotic (a simpler Egyptian script) and hieroglyphic. By comparison between the three inscriptions, a Frenchman, Jean-François Champollion, succeeded over twenty years later in eventually deciphering the hieroglyphs.

Over seven hundred hieroglyphic symbols are now understood. Those on the sweater are pure decoration, selected for their interesting abstract shapes rather than their true meaning. But if any knitters start to decipher the signs they will find among them ∿∿∿ , the sign for water, and ☞ , taken from the sign for the eye of Horus, the Egyptian falcon-god. The Egyptians themselves are not known to have used hieroglyphs as decoration on clothing, but signs such as the eye of Horus were used as amulets for their magical significance: according to myth, the eye was torn from Horus's head by the evil storm god, Seth, and was later miraculously restored to Horus by Thoth, the god of learning – thus the sign was thought to bring good health and luck to the wearer.

Tomb painting at Deir-el-Medineh showing the god of the dead, Osiris. The god wears an elaborate head-dress and deep, decorative collar and is flanked by the eye of Horus. In the foreground are an altar and water-skins; the painting is surrounded by hieroglyphic symbols.

EGYPTIAN SWEATER

VERSION 1 🧶🧶🧶

MATERIALS
Yarn
Use double-knit weight: 650(750)g/23(27) oz cream (A), 50g(2oz) blue (B), 25g(1oz) each of yellow (C), green (D), black (E), rust (F), brown (G)

Needles
1 pair each of 3¾mm (US 5) and 4½mm (US 7) needles

Tension
20 sts and 26 rows to 10cm (4in) on 4½mm needles and st st.

NOTES
• Any double-knit weight yarn can be used, whether cotton or wool, as long as the tension is the same as that given.

• When working the motifs, wind off small amounts of the required colours so that each motif can be worked separately, twisting yarns around each other on wrong side at joins to avoid holes. Yarn can be carried over wrong side over not more than 3 sts at a time to keep fabric elastic.

BACK
With 3¾mm needles and A, cast on 100(110) sts and work in double rib as follows:
Row 1: (RS facing) K0(2), *P2, K2, rep from * to end.
Row 2: *P2, K2, rep from * to last 0(2) sts, P0(2).
Rep last 2 rows until rib measures 10cm (4in) ending with a 2nd row. Change to 4½mm needles and work in st st from chart (see overleaf for charts), working decs for raglan shaping as indicated until row 138(144) has been worked. Cast off rem 20(22) sts.

FRONT
Work as for back until row 118 (124) of chart has been worked.
Shape front neck
Next row: (RS facing – following chart) Patt 17 sts, cast off centre 12(14) sts, patt to end of row, and cont on this last set of sts only. ** Keeping raglan decs as set, dec 1 st at neck edge on foll 4 alt rows. Keeping neck edge straight, cont to dec at raglan edge until all sts are worked. Fasten off. With WS facing rejoin yarn to rem sts and work as for first side from ** to end.

SLEEVES
Make 2. With 3¾mm needles and A, cast on 48(58) sts and work in double rib as for back welt for 10cm (4in) ending with a 2nd row and inc 1 st at each end of last rib row only – 50(60)sts. Change to 4½mm needles and work in st st from chart, reading chart as for back, and working inc rows as indicated at each end of 3rd row and then every foll 3rd row until there are 98(108) sts. Cont to follow chart working raglan decs at each

MEASUREMENTS (see also page 167)

Two sizes	small-medium	medium-large
To fit bust:	81–91cm (32–36in)	91–102cm (36–40in)
Actual measurement:	100cm (39½in)	110cm (43½in)
Length from back neck:	63cm (25in)	65cm (25¾in)
Sleeve seam:	42cm (16½in)	42cm (16½in)

end of row 83 and then rows as indicated until row 142(148) has been worked. Cast off rem 8(10) sts. Sew in all ends and press all pieces lightly on wrong side following ball band instructions.

RAGLAN RIBS
4 alike (these are worked along the top shaped edges of the sleeves). With 3¾mm needles and A, and RS facing, pick up and K 60(66) sts along one side of shaped raglan sleeve edge and work in double rib as for back welt for 10 rows.
Cast off loosely in rib.

NECKBAND
Join raglan seams leaving left back raglan open. With 3¾mm needles and A, and RS facing, pick up and K5 sts along top edge of left raglan rib, 8 sts at top left sleeve, 5 sts along raglan rib, 37(39) sts around front neck, 5 sts along raglan rib, 8 sts at top right sleeve, 5 sts along raglan rib and 19(21) sts at back neck – 92(96) sts.
Work in double rib for 7.5cm (3in).
Cast off in rib using a 4½mm needle.

TO MAKE UP
Join remaining raglan seam and neckband. Join side and sleeve seams. Press seams. Fold neckband in half to outside and stitch down carefully.

VERSION 2 🧶🧶

WORKED IN TWO COLOURS ONLY

MATERIALS
Yarn
Use double-knit weight: 650(750)g/23(27)oz cream (A), 125(5oz) green (B)
Needles and tension as for Version 1.

METHOD
This version is worked exactly as for Version 1, but in two colours only substituting the contrast colour B for yarns B, C, D, E, F and G on the original chart. The background colour A remains the same.

VERSION 3 🧶

WORKED IN ONE COLOUR ONLY

MATERIALS
Yarn
Use double-knit weight: 750(850)g/27(30)oz chosen colour
Needles and tension as for Version 1.

METHOD
Work as for Version 1 in one colour only omitting all motifs.

opposite
Version 1: Egyptian raglan sweater knitted in cream cotton with coloured 'hieroglyph' motifs, worn with a beaded, multicoloured collar.

EGYPTIAN SWEATER BACK AND FRONT CHART

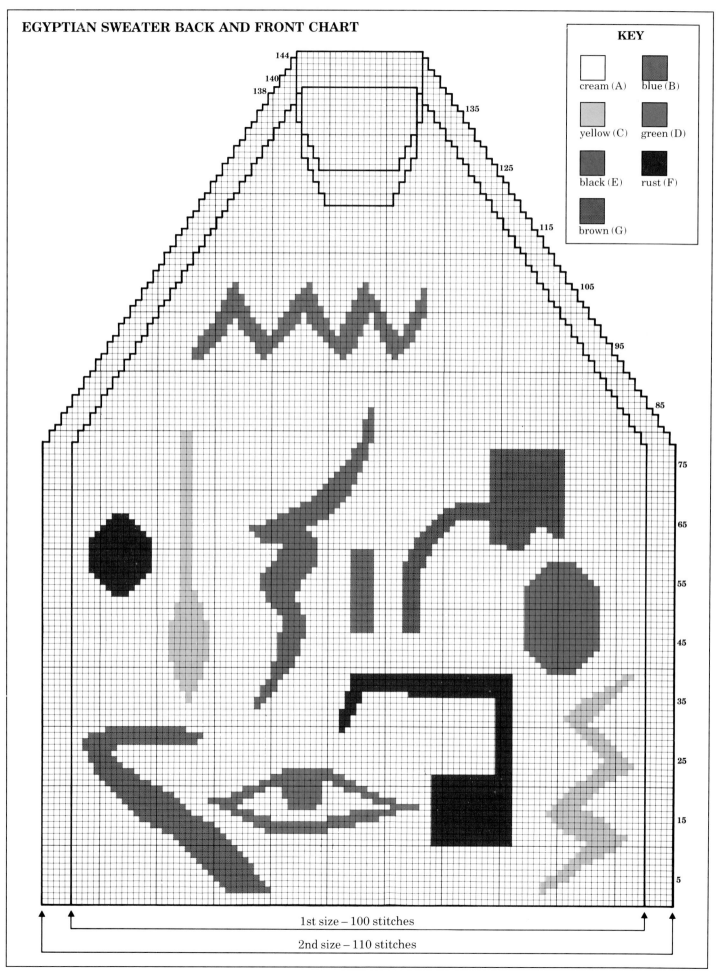

KEY

cream (A)   blue (B)

yellow (C)   green (D)

black (E)   rust (F)

brown (G)

1st size – 100 stitches

2nd size – 110 stitches

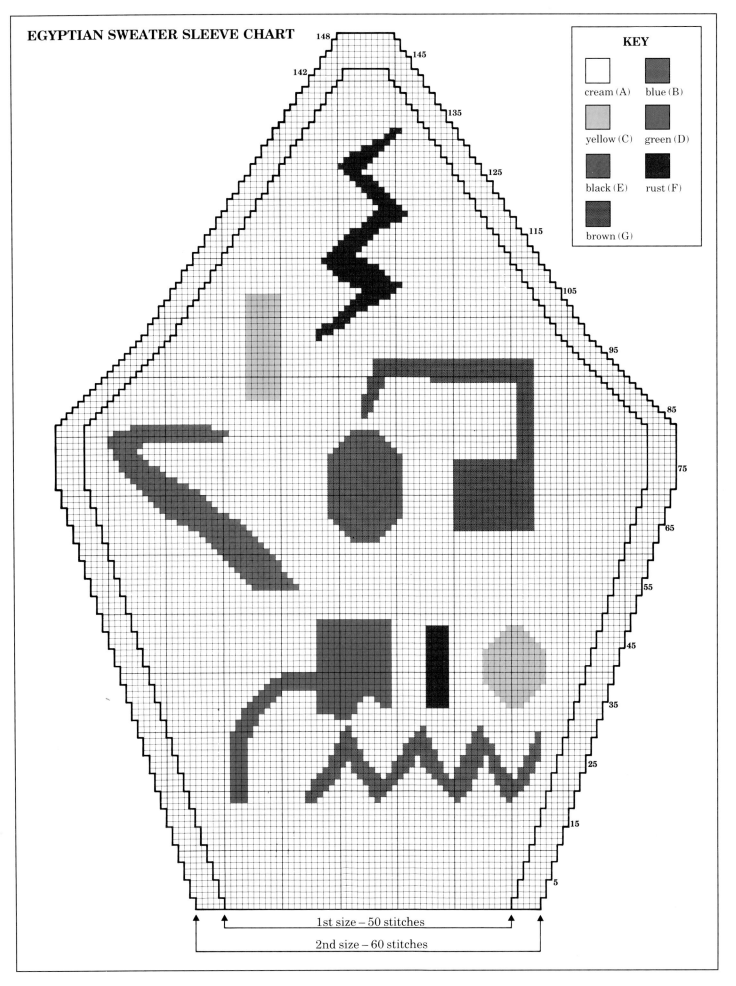

EGYPTIAN SWEATER SLEEVE CHART

KEY

cream (A) blue (B)

yellow (C) green (D)

black (E) rust (F)

brown (G)

148
145
142
135
125
115
105
95
85
75
65
55
45
35
25
15
5

1st size – 50 stitches

2nd size – 60 stitches

15

Variations on Version 1.

Version 2: the 'hieroglyph' sweater knitted in cream and green with matching collar.

Version 3: plain black raglan sweater worn with a striped collar.

EGYPTIAN COLLAR

MEASUREMENTS (see also page 167)

To fit one size.	
Approx bottom width:	120cm (47¼in)
Length:	20cm (8in)

VERSION 1

MATERIALS
Yarn
Use double-knit weight: 25g (1oz) each of cream (A), blue (B), yellow (C), green (D), rust (F), brown (G); 100g (4oz) black (E)

Needles and other materials
1 pair each of 3¾mm (US 5) and 4½mm (US 7) needles, 1 4½mm (US 7) circular needle
Crochet hook, 1 button

For decoration
120 gold drop beads
60 flat round multicolour beads
50 round beads
102cm (40in) yarn lengths: 2 × gold lurex, 1 × black (E), 1 × rust (F), 1 × blue (B)
76cm (30in) yarn lengths: 2 × gold lurex, 1 × black (E), 1 × rust (F), 1 × blue (B)

Tension
20 sts and 26 rows to 10cm (4in) on 4½mm needles and st st.

NOTES
● Any double-knit weight yarn can be used, whether cotton or wool, as long as the tension is the same as that given.

● When working from chart strand yarn on wrong side of work over not more than 3 sts at a time to keep fabric elastic. Collar is worked in rows on a circular needle because of the amount of stitches required, but it is *not* worked in the round.

METHOD
With the 4½mm circular needle and E, cast on 240 sts and work 3 rows in g st (every row K).
Now work in st st, repeating the 8 stitch patt from chart until row 10 has been worked.

Shape collar
Next row: (row 11 of chart) *K4, K2 tog, rep from * to end, keeping chart correct – 200 sts.
Cont repeating appropriate sts of chart until row 20 has been worked.
Next row: (row 21 of chart) *K3, K2 tog, rep from * to end, keeping chart correct – 160 sts.
Cont repeating appropriate sts of chart until row 28 has been worked.
Next row: (row 29 of chart) *K2, K2 tog, rep from * to end, keeping chart correct – 120 sts.
Cont repeating appropriate sts of chart until row 38 has been worked.
Next row: (row 39 of chart) *K3, K2 tog, rep from * to end, keeping chart correct – 96 sts.
Row 40: P in G.
With RS facing, K1 row in E.

Neck ribbing
Change to 3¾mm needles and E and work 10 rows in K1, P1, rib.
Cast off loosely in rib.

TO MAKE UP
Sew in all ends. Gently press collar, except for neck ribbing, on reverse side according to ball band instructions.
Fold neck ribbing in half to outside and stitch down carefully to give a neat neck edging.

Side collar edging
Alike (Diagram 1). With 4½mm needles and E, with RS facing, pick up and K 36 sts evenly along one collar side edge and work 3 rows in g st. Cast off.

Button loop
(Diagram 2), with the crochet hook and E, make a button loop at neck edge on left side of collar. Sew on a button to correspond with button loop.

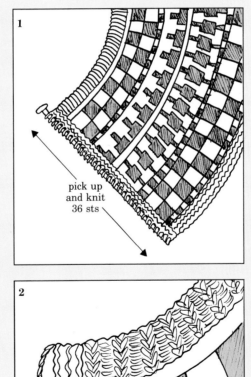

pick up and knit 36 sts

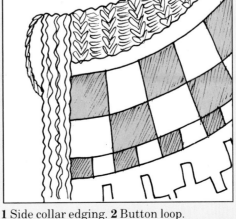

1 Side collar edging. 2 Button loop.

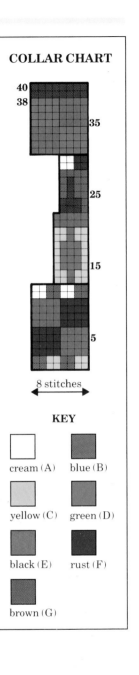

COLLAR CHART

40
38
35
25
15
5

8 stitches

KEY

cream (A)	blue (B)
yellow (C)	green (D)
black (E)	rust (F)
brown (G)	

DECORATION

Sew on beads as illustrated **(Diagram 3)**.
Knot the 102cm yarn lengths together at one end
and push the knot through to the back of the
collar at the beginning of rows 21 and 22 and
stitch knot down neatly **(Diagram 4)**. Now twist
the yarns around each other a few cm at a time.
Lay the cord on the collar along rows 21 and 22,
pinning it in place **(Diagram 5)**. Stab stitch cord
onto collar moving pins along as you work. When
you reach the end make another knot and push
through the collar to the back and stitch down
neatly. A second cord is made with the 76cm yarn
lengths and is worked along row 39 in exactly the
same way.

VERSION 2

WORKED IN TWO COLOURS ONLY

MATERIALS
Yarn
Use double-knit weight: 125g(5oz) green (A),
100g(4oz) cream (B)

Needles and tension as for Version 1.

METHOD
Follow instructions for Version 1, but using only
two colours as follows:
For yarns B, D and F substitute B above. For
yarns A, C, E and G substitute A above.

VERSION 3

STRIPED COLLAR

MATERIALS
Yarn
Use double-knit weight: 25g(1oz) each of cream
(A), blue (B), yellow (C), rust (D); 100g(4oz)
black (E)
Needles and tension as for Version 1.

METHOD
With the circular 4½mm needle and E, cast on
240 sts and work 3 rows in g st (every row K).
Then work as follows:
Row 1: K in B.
Row 2: P in B.
Rows 3-10: Work in st st in D.
Row 11: With A, *K4, K2 tog, rep from * to end –
200 sts.
Row 12: P in A.
Rows 13-20: Work in st st in C.
Row 21: With E, *K3, K2 tog, rep from * to end –
160 sts.
Row 22: P in E.
Rows 23-28: Work in st st in B.
Row 29: With D, *K2, K2 tog, rep from * to end –
120 sts.
Row 30: P in D.
Rows 31-38 Work in st st in A.
Row 39: With C, *K3, K2 tog, rep from * to end –
96 sts.
Row 40: P in C.
Now complete as for Version 1.

NOTE
● Versions 2 and 3 of the collar can be left
plain or can be decorated with beads and
braid as required.

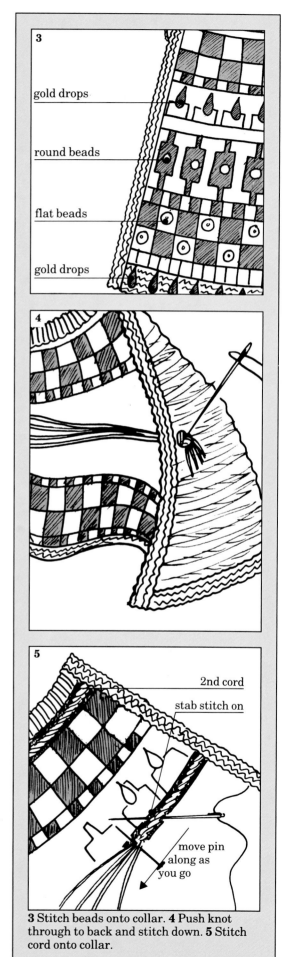

3 Stitch beads onto collar. 4 Push knot
through to back and stitch down. 5 Stitch
cord onto collar.

EGYPTIAN CARDIGAN

MEASUREMENTS (see also page 167)

Three sizes	small	medium	large
To fit bust:	81-91cm(32-36in)	91-102cm(36-40in)	102-112cm(40-44in)
Actual measurement:	101cm(39¾in)	108.5cm(42¾in)	116cm(45¾in)
Length from shoulder:	70cm(27½in)	73cm(28¾in)	75cm(29½in)
Sleeve seam:	51cm(20in)	53cm(21in)	56cm(22in)

VERSION 1

MATERIALS

Yarn
Use double-knit weight: 500(550 : 600)g/18 (20 : 22)oz cream viscose (A), 50(50 : 75)g/2(2 : 3)oz rust wool (B), 75(75 : 100)g/3 (3 : 4)oz each royal blue wool (C), turquoise wool (D), 75(100 : 125)g/3(4 : 5)oz gold lurex worked double (E), 50g(2oz) each ochre wool (F), brown cotton (G)

Needles and other materials
1 pair each of 3¼mm (US 3), 4mm (US 6) and 3¾mm (US 5) needles
2 safety pins, 9 pearl buttons
For decoration
34 gold beads

Tension
22 sts and 28 rows to 10cm (4in) on 4mm needles and st st using viscose yarn.

> **NOTES**
> • Any double-knit weight yarn can be used, as long as the tension is the same as that given.
> • The gold lurex should be worked *double* throughout.

BACK
With 3¼mm needles and A, cast on 84(90 : 96) sts and work in double rib as follows:
Row 1: (RS facing) K0(2 : 0), *P2, K2, rep from * to end.
Row 2: *P2, K2, rep from * to last 0(2 : 0)sts, P0(2 : 0).
Rep last 2 rows for 15cm (6in), ending with a 1st row.
Increase row: Rib and inc 1 st in every 3rd st across row – 112(120 : 128)sts.

Change to 4mm needles and using A, and starting with a K row, work straight in st st until back measures 43(46 : 48)cm/17 (18 : 19)in from cast-on edge, ending with a WS row.
Now work in st st from **Chart 1** as follows:
On **section A,** work the 8-stitch patt repeat between the dotted lines 14(15 : 16) times across row.
Cont as set until row 30 of chart has been worked (**section A** is now complete). Now work from **section B** as follows:
Starting with a K row (row 31) work 2(0 : 4)sts before the dotted line, rep the 12-stitch patt between the dotted lines 9(10 : 10) times across

row, work 2(0 : 4)sts beyond the dotted line. On P rows, work likewise. Cont as set until row 70 of chart has been worked.
Shape shoulders (row 71)
Keeping chart correct, cast off 9(10 : 11)sts at beg of next 8 rows. Cast off rem 40 sts.

RIGHT FRONT
**With 3¼mm needles and A, cast on 36(40 : 42)sts and work in double rib as follows:
Row 1: (RS facing) K0(0 : 2), *P2, K2, rep from * to end.
Row 2: *P2, K2, rep from * to last 0(0 : 2)sts, P0(0 : 2).
Rep last 2 rows for 15cm (6in), ending with a 1st row.
Increase row: Rib and inc 1 st in every 2nd st across row – 54(60 : 63)sts.
Change to 4mm needles and using A, starting with a K row, work straight in st st: on **1st size only** inc 1 st at each end of 1st row, on **3rd size only** inc 1 st at beg of 1st row – 56(60 : 64)sts.
Now work in st st until front measures the same as back to beg of chart, ending with a WS row.**
Now work in st st from **Chart 2** (see page 23) as follows:
Start on **section A,** and on K rows rep the 8-stitch patt between the dotted lines 7(7 : 8) times across row to last 0(4 : 0)sts, work 0(4 : 0)sts beyond the dotted line. On P rows work 0(4 : 0)sts before the dotted line, then rep the 8-stitch patt 7(7 : 8) times across row. Cont to follow **section A** as now set until row 24 has been worked. Now place **sections B and C** as follows:
Next row: (RS facing) K8F, now work across the 14 sts of row 1 of **section B,** K10F, now work across the 20 sts of row 1 of **section C,** K4(8 : 12)F.
Next row: P4(8 : 12)F, now work across the 20 sts of row 2 of **section C,** P10F, now work across the 14 sts on row 2 of **section B,** P8F.
These 2 rows place the pattern.
Cont as now set, repeating the 8 rows of **section B** and the 10 rows of **section C** as required.
Cont straight in patt as now set until front measures 64(67 : 69)cm/25(26¼ : 27)in from cast-on edge, ending with a WS row.
Shape front neck
Keeping patts correct, cast off 8 sts at beg of next row. Now dec 1 st at neck edge on next row and 11 foll rows – 36(40 : 44)sts.
Now work a few rows straight in patt until front measures the same as back to start of shoulder shaping, ending at side edge.
Shape shoulder
Keeping patts correct, cast off 9(10 : 11)sts at beg of next row and 3 foll alt rows.

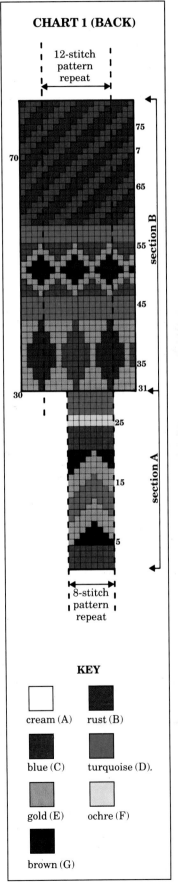

CHART 1 (BACK)

12-stitch pattern repeat

75
7
70
65
55
45
35
31
30
25
15
5

section B
section A

8-stitch pattern repeat

KEY

cream (A)   rust (B)

blue (C)   turquoise (D).

gold (E)   ochre (F)

brown (G)

LEFT FRONT

Work as for right front from ** to **.
Start on **section A** and on K rows work 0(4 : 0)sts before the dotted line, then rep the 8-stitch patt between the dotted lines 7(7 : 8) times across row. On P rows rep the 8-stitch patt between the dotted lines 7(7 : 8) times across row to last 0(4 : 0)sts, work 0(4 : 0)sts beyond the dotted line. Cont to follow **section A** as now set until row 24 has been worked.
Now place **sections B** and **C** as follows:
Next row: (RS facing) K4(8 : 12)F, now work across the 20 sts of row 1 of **section C,** K10F, now work across the 14 sts of row 1 of **section B,** K8F. This row places the patt.
Now cont as for right front, working patt as now placed and reversing all shapings.

SLEEVES

Make 2. With 3¾mm needles and D, cast on 44(48 : 52)sts and work in K1, P1, rib for 4 rows.
Change to 4mm needles and work in st st from **Chart 3 (cuff)** as follows:
On K rows work 4(0 : 2) sts before the dotted line, rep the 12-stitch patt 3(4 : 4) times across row, work 4(0 : 2)sts beyond the dotted line. On P rows work likewise.
Cont as set until the 16 rows of chart have been worked.
Next row: (RS facing) K in D.
Change to 3¼mm needles and work in K1, P1, rib in D for 3 rows.
Break off all contrast yarns and cont in A only.
Change to 4mm needles.
Increase row: (RS facing) K and inc 1 st in every 2nd st across row – 66(72 : 78)sts.
Starting with a P row, cont in st st and inc 1 st at beg of every row until there are 122(130 : 138)sts on the needle.
Work straight in st st until sleeve measures 31(33 : 36)cm/12(13 : 14)in from cast-on edge, ending with a WS row.
Now place pattern and work in st st from **Chart 3 (top sleeve)** as follows:
1st size only, 1st row: Start on 5th st in from dotted line and work to 2nd dotted line, then rep the 24-stitch patt 4 times across row, work 6 sts beyond the dotted line.
2nd size only, 1st row: Rep the 24-stitch patt between the dotted lines 5 times, work 10 sts beyond the dotted line.
3rd size only, 1st row: Work 4 sts before the dotted line, rep the 24-stitch patt 5 times across row, work 14 sts beyond the dotted line.
All sizes: This row places the patt.
Cont in patt as set until the 54 rows of chart have been worked.
Cast off in D.

TO MAKE UP

Sew in all ends and press pieces lightly on wrong side following ball band instructions.
Join shoulder seams. With centre of cast-off edges of sleeves to shoulder seams, position sleeves, reaching down to same depth on back and front. Sew in position. Join side and sleeve seams.

Buttonhole band

With 3¼mm needles and A, cast on 10 sts, and work in K1, P1, rib for 1cm(½in), ending with a WS row.
Next row: (buttonhole row) Rib 4, cast off 3 sts, rib to end.

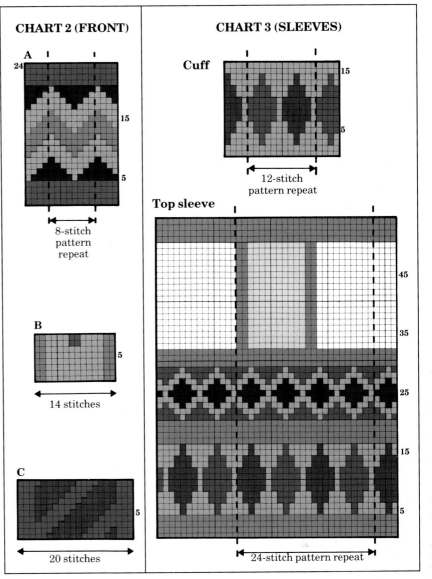

CHART 2 (FRONT)

A

8-stitch pattern repeat

B

14 stitches

C

20 stitches

CHART 3 (SLEEVES)

Cuff

12-stitch pattern repeat

Top sleeve

24-stitch pattern repeat

Next row: Rib 3, cast on 3 sts, rib to end.
Now cont in rib, making 7 further buttonholes at 8(8.5 : 9)cm/3(3½ : 3¾)in intervals from previous buttonhole. Work in rib for a further 7(6.5 : 5)cm/2¾(2½ : 2)in. Leave sts on a safety pin. (8 buttonholes made in all.)

Button band

Work to match buttonhole band omitting buttonholes.
Attach bands to centre front edges with buttonhole band to right front.

Collar

One size. With 4mm needles and E and RS facing, and starting where the right front band joins the right front, pick up and K 30 sts from centre front to shoulder seam, 36 sts across back neck and 30 sts from shoulder seam to where left front band joins the left front – 96 sts
(**Diagram 1** see page 24).
With WS facing and starting with a K row work in Fair Isle pattern as follows:
Row 1: (RS of collar facing) K in E.
Row 2: P in E.
Row 3: *K3C, K3B, rep from * to end.
Row 4: *P3B, P3C, rep from * to end.
Row 5: As row 3.
Row 6: As row 4.

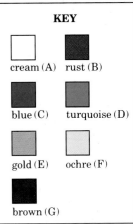

KEY

cream (A)   rust (B)

blue (C)   turquoise (D)

gold (E)   ochre (F)

brown (G)

opposite
Version 1: Egyptian cardigan knitted in cream viscose with the yoke, collar and cuffs patterned in blue, turquoise, rust, ochre, brown and gold. The yoke and top of the sleeves are decorated with gold beads.

23

Row 7: K in E, inc 1 st in every 3rd st across row – 128 sts.
Row 8: P in E.
Row 9: K3D, *K1E, K5D, rep from * to last 5 sts, K1E, K4D.
Row 10: P4D, *P1E, P5D, rep from * to last 4 sts, P1E, P3D.
Row 11: K2D, *K3E, K3D, rep from * to end.
Row 12: *P3D, P1E, P1B, P1E, rep from * to last 2 sts, P2D.
Row 13: *K1D, K2E, K1B, K2E, rep from * to last 2 sts, K2D.
Row 14: *P1E, P1D, P1E, P3B, rep from * to last 2 sts, P1E, P1D.
Row 15: K2E, *K3B, K3E, rep from * to end.
Row 16: P1B, *P1E, P5B, rep from * to last st, P1E.
Row 17: *K1E, K5B, rep from * to last 2 sts, K1E, K1B.
Row 18: P in B.
Row 19: K in A, inc 1 st in every 2nd st across row – 192 sts.
Row 20: P in A.
Row 21: K3C, *K1E, K5C, rep from * to last 3 sts, K1E, K2C.
Row 22: P1C, *P3E, P3C, rep from * to last 5 sts, P3E, P2C.
Row 23: *K1C, K2E, K1G, K2E, rep from * to end.
Row 24: P1E, *P3G, P3E, rep from * to last 5 sts, P3G, P2E.
Row 25: *K1E, K5G, rep from * to end.
Row 26: As row 24.
Row 27: As row 23.
Row 28: As row 22.
Row 29: As row 21.
Now P 1 row in A.
Change to 4mm needles and work 1 row in K1, P1, rib in A.
Cast off loosely in rib in A.
Sew in all ends of collar and press lightly on wrong side.

Side collar edging
Alike (Diagram 2). With 3¾mm needles and A and RS facing, pick up and K 28 sts along one front side edge of collar. Work in K1, P1, rib for 1 row. Cast off in rib. Sew in ends.

Neck ribbing
(Diagram 3). With 3¾mm needles and A and RS facing, rib across the 10 sts of right front band, now pick up and K 30 sts to shoulder seam (pick up the sts along the top of the collar where it joins to neck edge) 32 sts across back neck, 30 sts to front band, rib across the 10 sts of 2nd front band – 112 sts.
Work in K1, P1, rib in A for 3 rows.
Next row: (RS facing – buttonhole row) Rib 4, cast off 3 sts, rib to end.
Next row: Rib to last 4 sts, cast on 3 sts, rib 4.
Work 6 rows in K1, P1, rib then, with RS facing, work another buttonhole as before.
Work 2 more rows in rib. Cast off in rib.
Fold neck ribbing in half to outside, matching buttonholes, and stitch down carefully. Oversew around buttonhole.
Sew on buttons to correspond with buttonholes.

DECORATION
Stitch beads onto front yoke and the tops of the sleeves as shown in **Diagram 4** (see page 26).

1 Version 1 collar. 2 Version 1 side collar edging. 3 Version 1 neck ribbing.

Version 2: Egyptian cardigan with rust as the main colour and a simple round neck.

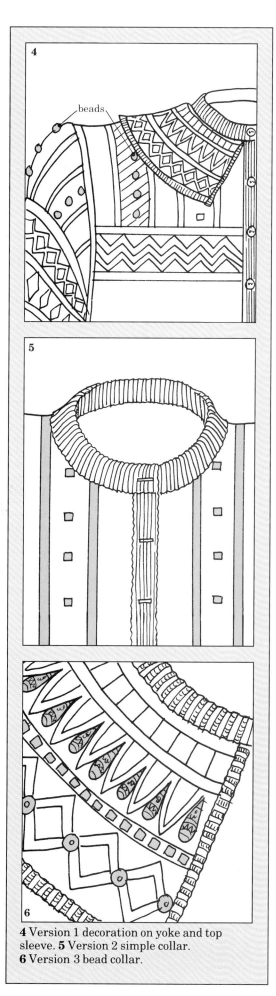

4 Version 1 decoration on yoke and top sleeve. **5** Version 2 simple collar.
6 Version 3 bead collar.

DECORATED EGYPTIAN CARDIGAN WITHOUT COLLAR

This version is worked exactly the same as Version 1. The needles and tension are the same, but the main background colour is changed by substituting yarn A for B and yarn B for A.

METHOD

Follow all instructions as for Version 1, but omit instructions for collar and move straight on to the neck ribbing instructions so that the cardigan has a simple round neck with no collar (**Diagram 5**).

VERSION 3

PLAIN CARDIGAN WITH DECORATED COLLAR AND PATTERNED CUFFS

MATERIALS

Yarn

Use double-knit weight: 800(850 : 900)g/29(30 : 32)oz cream viscose (A), 25g(1oz) each for all sizes of rust wool (B), royal blue wool (C), turquoise wool (D), gold lurex worked double (E), yellow wool (F) and brown cotton (G)
Needles and tension as for Version 1.

For decoration

35 round gold beads
25 fancy drop beads
60 beads in assorted colours

METHOD

In this version the garment has been simplified so that the main part of the knitting is in one colour. Follow instructions for Version 1 but instead of working in Fair Isle on the yokes, work in A in st st for required number of rows as on chart.
For the sleeves, work the decorative cuffs, and then work the rest of the sleeve in st st in A only.
Follow all the instructions for collar and neck ribbing but omit the bead decoration on the yokes and sleeves.

COLLAR DECORATION

The collar may be decorated with beads (**Diagram 6**).

Version 3: cream cardigan with patterned, beaded collar and patterned cuffs.

ANCIENT GREECE AND ROME
INTRODUCTION

Greek and Roman culture permeates the whole of Western civilization and is often seen as a single influence. But the characters of the two peoples were vastly different. The Greeks were imaginative innovators – artists, philosophers, mathematicians and poets; the Romans were more practical: engineers, law-givers, brilliant soldiers and administrators of their vast Empire. The two sweaters in this chapter express something of these contrasting identities.

Greek clothes changed little over the centuries and their flattering clean lines, so familiar from sculpture and the figures on Greek vases, were achieved simply by draping and pinning rectangles of cloth in a variety of ways. The universal garment was the *chiton,* a kind of tunic, which was usually worn knee-length by men and ankle-length by women. The earliest type of chiton, the Doric, originated in mainland Greece, and was made from wool, with a deep over-fold at the top, fastened at the shoulders with large *fibulae* or pins. The later Ionic chiton first developed in the Greek colonies of Asia Minor and was then adopted by the people of the mainland. Like the architectural style of the same name, the Ionic chiton was a more elegant and graceful garment than the Doric, usually made of linen or silk. Although elements of both styles were often combined in one garment, the Greek Dolman Sweater with its full sleeves (see photograph, page 31) is firmly based on the Ionic.

The fine linen or silk of the Ionic chiton could be arranged in graceful folds and sometimes reached voluminous proportions up to 3m (10 ft) wide. Cloth was woven in Grecian homes to the length that suited the wearer, rather than being cut later from a roll. Silk fibres were probably imported from Asia, but the majority of silk spinning was done on the island of Cos. The Ionic chiton had no top fold, but was fastened at intervals along the top edge by small brooches or buttons, and when it was belted loose sleeves were formed. In the typical Ionic chiton the armholes were in line with the neck on the top edge of the garment and this feature created the particularly attractive loose folds around the arms.

The statuesque quality of Greek dress inspired contemporary artists and sculptors who delighted in the skilful representation of every fold. On the caryatid figures which supported entablatures on buildings, ingenious use was made of sculptured folds to disguise the heavy line of the columns on the weight-bearing side. The Grecian look has often inspired later fashions – notably the diaphanous neo-classical designs of the early 1800s immortalized in portraits like *Madame Récamier* by David. In this century the Italian fashion designer Mariano Fortuny made finely-pleated dresses based on classical styles (the Greeks often pleated clothes with thin starch).

Soft grey viscose is used for the Greek Dolman Sweater: the silky texture recalling Grecian silk, the colour evoking the silver-grey leaves of an olive grove. The flattering loose shape and sleeves fastened at intervals are very close to the Ionic chiton of antiquity. Pale clear colours are used for the leaf motif on the yoke – leaves were a recurrent classical motif, which the Greeks sometimes used on clothes. They also wore wreaths in their hair, usually made from fresh leaves, but there are some beautiful examples made of beaten gold or silver with every leaf exquisitely wrought. Wreaths made of different kinds of leaf – olive, pine, laurel and palm – were awarded to victorious Olympic athletes and as prizes to poets and orators.

Although the Romans, too, favoured simple draped clothes, somehow their style of dress speaks more of military might and individual status. Again the main garment for both sexes was a tunic which was often made of wool; sometimes more than one of these was worn – the Italian climate was less certain than that of Greece and those in the northernmost outposts of the Empire would have needed plenty of protection from the elements.

The wool Roman Sweater (see photograph, page 37) is tunic-shaped with bold white, grey and silver decoration on a black background. On the yoke and sleeves the leaf motif appears again, but the broad shoulder bands and silver stud decoration recall the details of Roman armour and give a militaristic feel.

Silver coins add extra interest; Roman garments were probably never trimmed with coins, but coinage was an important instrument of Roman propaganda enabling the image of the current Emperor to be made known throughout the Empire. As a finishing touch, the centre of the yoke is adorned by a large rhinestone – the Romans loved rather ostentatious jewellery set with precious stones such as sapphires, emeralds and sometimes diamonds.

Perhaps the most well-known Roman garment is the toga, which is thought to be Etruscan in origin. This was a very large semi-circular piece of cloth, measuring sometimes as much as 5.6 × 2m (18½ × 7ft), worn over the tunic and draped around the body in a complicated and elaborate manner – an art in itself. In this most hierarchical of societies there was a multitude of toga designs for different occasions and positions in life: the ordinary dress of a Roman citizen was the toga *pura* or *virilis* of undecorated natural-coloured wool, while the purple, gold-embroidered toga *picta* was worn by victorious generals, emperors and consuls.

An Athenian red-figured wine cup (c.490-480BC) shows Triptolemos in his winged chariot receiving corn to carry to mankind. The pleats, folds and sleeve fastenings of the Ionic-style chitons can be clearly seen.

The accessory for this chapter, the Roman Toga (see photograph, page 41), is based on a design for a high-ranking individual. It is edged with a leaf motif and its medallion-like patterns on a black background suggest Roman mosaics. Although not of such massive proportions as the originals, the 'toga' still makes a wonderfully warm stole. It would be quite 'classically' correct to wear it with the Greek sweater, because the Greeks, too, wore enveloping wraps over their chitons.

A Roman denarius (c. 211-208BC), a small silver coin which was the basic currency of the Roman Republic.

GREEK DOLMAN SWEATER

MEASUREMENTS (see also page 167)

Three sizes	small	medium	large
To fit bust:	81-91cm (32-36in)	91-102cm (36-40in)	102-112cm (40-44in)
Total width across front (excluding cuffs):	124cm (49in)	129cm (51in)	134cm (53in)
Length from shoulder:	74cm (29in)	74cm (29in)	74cm (29in)

VERSION 1

opposite
Version 1: 'Greek' dolman sweater knitted in grey viscose has a yoke decorated with a laurel-leaf motif; the sleeves are fastened at intervals by silver buttons and the cuffs match the yoke.

KEY

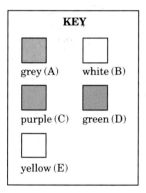

grey (A)   white (B)

purple (C)   green (D)

yellow (E)

MATERIALS

Yarn
Use double-knit weight: 675(725 : 775)g/24(26 : 28)oz grey viscose (A), 50g(2oz) each white cotton (B), purple cotton (C), yellow linen (E), 25g (1oz) green cotton (D)

Needles and other materials
1 pair each of 3¾mm (US 5) and 4½mm (US 7) needles, 1 circular 4½mm (US 7) needle
14 silver buttons or large beads for shoulders
Embroidery needle.

Tension
21 sts and 26 rows to 10cm (4in) on 4½mm needles over st st.

FRONT

With 3¾mm needles and A, cast on 80(92 : 100)sts and work in K2, P2 rib for 15cm (6in).
Increase row: Rib and inc 28(28 : 32) sts evenly across row – 108(120 : 132) sts.
Change to 4½mm needles and starting with a K row cont in st st in A as follows:
Row 1: (RS facing) Work straight.

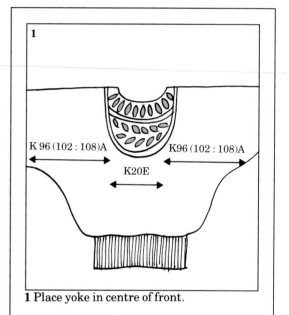

1 Place yoke in centre of front.

Row 2: Inc 1 st at each end of row.
Row 3: Inc 1 st at each end of row.
Keeping st st correct, rep these 3 rows until there are 214(226 : 238)sts on the needle, changing to the 4½mm circular needle when necessary, and ending with a WS row (80 rows of st st worked – front measures approx 46cm (18in) from cast-on edge).

Place yoke
Next row: (Row 1 of chart) Inc in 1st st, K96(102 : 108)A, K20E, K96 (102 : 108)A, inc in last st **(Diagram 1)**.
This row places the chart.
Keeping incs as set, cont to follow the chart until there are 258(270 : 282) sts on the needle (front measures approx 58cm (23in) from cast-on edge). Now keeping side edges straight, cont on these sts until row 48 of chart has been worked.

NOTES

- Any double-knit weight yarn can be used as long as the tension is the same as that given above.

- When working from chart, strand yarn not in use loosely across the wrong side of work over not more than 3 sts at a time to keep fabric elastic.

- A circular needle is used because of the amount of stitches required, but the sweater is *not* worked in the round.

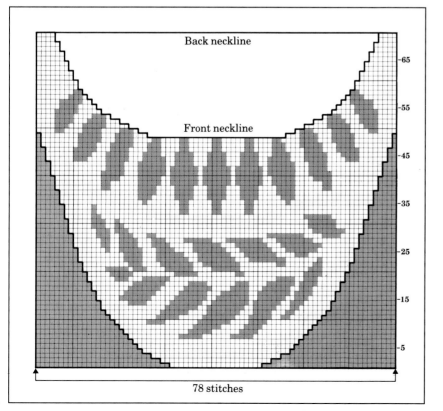

Back neckline

Front neckline

78 stitches

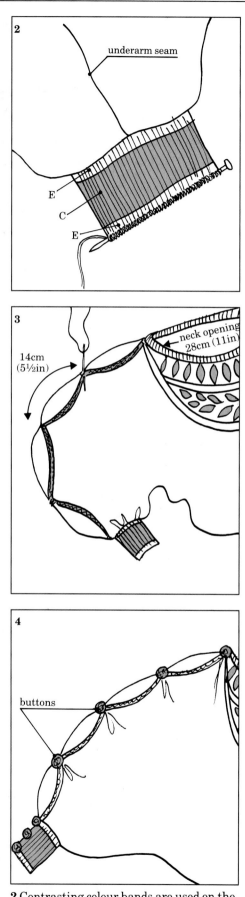

2 Contrasting colour bands are used on the cuffs. **3** Join shoulder seams at intervals of 14cm (5½in). **4** Decorate shoulder openings and cuffs with silver buttons.

Shape front neck
Next row: (RS facing) Patt 114(120 : 126)sts, cast off centre 30 sts and patt to end of row. Cont on the last set of 114(120 : 126)sts only.
****Dec 2 sts at neck edge on next row and 4 foll rows, then dec 1 st on this edge on next 5 rows, and then 1 st on foll 5 alt rows – 94(100 : 106)sts. Patt 1 row (row 70 of chart has now been worked).
Next row: (RS facing) K4E, K90(96 : 102)A.
Next row: K90(96 : 102)A, K4E.
Rep these 2 rows once more.
Cast off in colours as given.
With WS facing rejoin yarn to neck edge and work as for first side from ** to end.

BACK
Work exactly as for front but in A only until there are 258(270 : 282)sts on the needle, omitting chart.
Cont straight until back measures the same as front to shoulder edge, ending with a WS row.
K 4 rows
Cast off.

Sew in all ends and press pieces carefully paying special attention to the Fair Isle yoke.

FRONT NECK RIBBING
With 3¾mm needles and E and RS facing, pick up and K 26 sts down left side of front neck, 28 sts across centre front and 26 sts up right side of front neck – (80 sts).
Work 4 rows in K1, P1 rib in E.
Cast off neatly in rib.
Join both underarm seams. Press seams.

CUFFS
Alike. With 3¾mm needles and E and RS facing, pick up and K 40 sts along bottom edge of one sleeve (**Diagram 2**).
Work 4 rows in K1, P1 rib in E.
Work 7cm (2¾in) in K1, P1 rib in C.
Work 4 rows in K1, P1 rib in E.
Cast off loosely in rib in E.

TO MAKE UP
Stitch cuff seams together. Join shoulder seams at intervals of 14cm (5½in), leaving a gap of approx 28cm (11in) at centre for neck opening (**Diagram 3**).
Decorate shoulder openings and cuffs with large silver beads or buttons (**Diagram 4**).
Embroider a line of chain stitch in C along centre of leaf motifs on yoke (**Diagram 5** see page 34).

Version 2: the same dolman style knitted in white with yoke motif and cuffs picked out in black; pearls, silver beads and rhinestones are used for decoration.

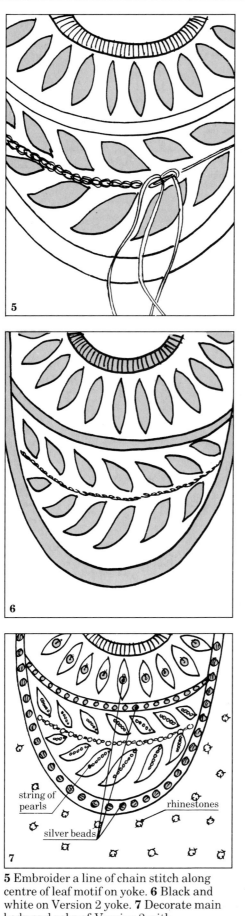

5 Embroider a line of chain stitch along centre of leaf motif on yoke. 6 Black and white on Version 2 yoke. 7 Decorate main body and yoke of Version 2 with rhinestones, silver beads and pearls.

VERSION 2

IN TWO COLOURS DECORATED WITH BEADS AND RHINESTONES

MATERIALS
Yarn
Use double-knit weight: 750(775 : 800)g/27(28 : 29)oz white (A), 75g(3oz) black (B)
Needles and tension as for Version 1.
For decoration
1 metre pearls on string
300 clear rhinestones
40 large silver beads
20 small silver beads

METHOD
Follow instructions for Version 1 but using white for main colour A.
Use black and white on decorative yolk (see **Diagram 6** for position of colours).
On cuffs substitute B for E and A for C.
Decorate yoke and main body of garment with rhinestones and beads (**Diagram 7**).

VERSION 3

PLAIN DOLMAN SWEATER

MATERIALS
Yarn
Use double-knit weight: 775(825 : 875)g/28(30 : 31)oz yellow linen (A)
Needles and tension as for Version 1.

METHOD
Follow instructions as for Version 1 but work whole garment in A.
Work from chart for front neck shaping but omit all motifs.
When making up, join complete shoulder seam and cuff together, instead of leaving openings on the shoulders.
The garment can still be decorated with buttons or beads across shoulder seams if desired.

Version 3: completely plain dolman sweater in yellow linen has conventional fully sewn-up sleeve seams and is worn with the grey and white Version 3 of the toga.

ROMAN SWEATER

MEASUREMENTS (see also page 168)

Two sizes	small-medium	medium-large
To fit bust:	81-91cm (32-36in)	91-97cm (36-38in)
Actual measurement:	105cm (41½in)	110cm (43¼in)
Length from shoulder:	73cm (29in)	73cm (29in)
Sleeve seam:	41cm (16in)	41cm (16in)

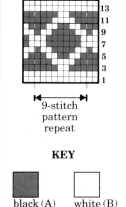

CHART 1

13
11
9
7
5
3
1

9-stitch
pattern
repeat

KEY

black (A)   white (B)

VERSION 1

MATERIALS

Yarn
Use double-knit: 400(450)g/15(16)oz black (A), 150g(6oz) white (B), 25g(1oz) each grey (C), silver lurex worked double (D)

Needles
1 pair each of 3¼mm (US 3) and 4mm (US 6) needles

For decoration
100 silver beads
70 silver sew-on coins
50 silver metal studs
1 large clear rhinestone

Tension
23 sts and 28 rows to 10cm (4in) on 4mm needles over st st.

NOTES

- Any double-knit weight yarn can be used as long as the tension is the same as that given above.

- The silver should be worked *double* throughout.

- It is easier to decorate the pieces flat before sewing them together.

- When working from charts, where possible, strand yarn not in use loosely across wrong side of work over not more than 3 sts at a time to keep fabric elastic. When working larger areas of one colour, use separate balls of yarn, twisting yarns around each other on wrong side at joins to avoid holes.

FRONT
With 3¼mm needles and A, cast on 100(108)sts and work in K1, P1 rib for 13cm (5in).
Increase row: Rib and inc 18 sts evenly across row – 118(126)sts.
Change to 4mm needles and work in st st from **Chart 1** as follows:
On K rows, work 1(0)st before the dotted line, rep the 9-stitch patt between the dotted lines to end of row. On P rows, work the 9-stitch patt across row to last 1(0)st, work 1(0)st beyond the dotted line. Work as set until the 14 rows of chart are complete. Now cont in A only and work straight in st st for a further 42 rows, thus ending with a WS row.
Now work from **Chart 2** (see page 38), working between appropriate lines for size required, until row 38 has been worked.

Shape armholes
Rows 39 and 40: Cast off 10 sts at beg of next 2 rows.
Now keeping chart correct, cast off 1 st at each end of next row and then every foll alt row until 90 sts remain.
Cont to follow chart until row 84 has been worked.

Shape front neck
Row 85: Patt 26 sts, cast off centre 38 sts and patt to end, and cont on this last set of 26 sts only for first side. Patt 1 row.
**Keeping chart correct, dec 1 st at beg (neck edge) of next row and at this edge on every foll alt row, until 21 sts remain.
Cont straight following chart until row 109 has been worked.

Shape shoulder
Row 110: Cast off 7 sts at beg of next and 2 foll alt rows.
With WS facing rejoin yarn to rem sts and work as for first side from ** to end, noting that shoulder shaping starts on row 109.

BACK
Work as for front until the completion of the border pattern. Now cont in A only and follow **Chart 2** (omitting all motifs) shaping armholes as for front.
Omit front neck shaping and cont straight on the 90 sts until row 108 of chart has been worked.

Shape shoulders
Cast off 7 sts at beg of next 6 rows. Cast off rem 48 sts for back neck.

SLEEVES
Make 2. Decorative cuff: With 3¼mm needles and B, cast on 40(46)sts and work in K1, P1 rib for 2 rows.
Now work in st st from **Chart 1** starting from Row 3, and work K rows by working 2(1) st(s) before the dotted line, rep the 9-stitch patt between the dotted lines to last 2(0)sts, work 2(0) sts beyond the dotted line. On P rows, work 2(0) sts before the dotted line, rep the 9-stitch patt between the dotted lines to last 2(1)st(s), work 2(1) st(s) beyond the dotted line.
Work as set until the chart is complete, now work in A only.
Increase row: (RS facing) K and inc 30(32)sts evenly across row – 70(78)sts.
Change to 4mm needles and starting with a P row, work 2 rows in st st.
Now inc 1 st at both ends of next row and then every foll 3rd row until there are 94(102) sts on the needle.
Work 2 rows in st st, thus ending with a WS row.
Now work from **Chart 3** (see page 39), working between appropriate lines for size required, inc 1 st at each end of 1st row and then every foll 3rd row as set, until there are 112(120)sts on the needle. Cont to follow chart until row 52 has been worked.

opposite
Version 1: black is used for the background of the dramatic Roman sweater; the contrast patterning is in white, silver and grey; silver coins, beads and studs highlight the motifs and a large rhinestone adorns the centre of the yoke.

CHART 2 (BACK/FRONT)

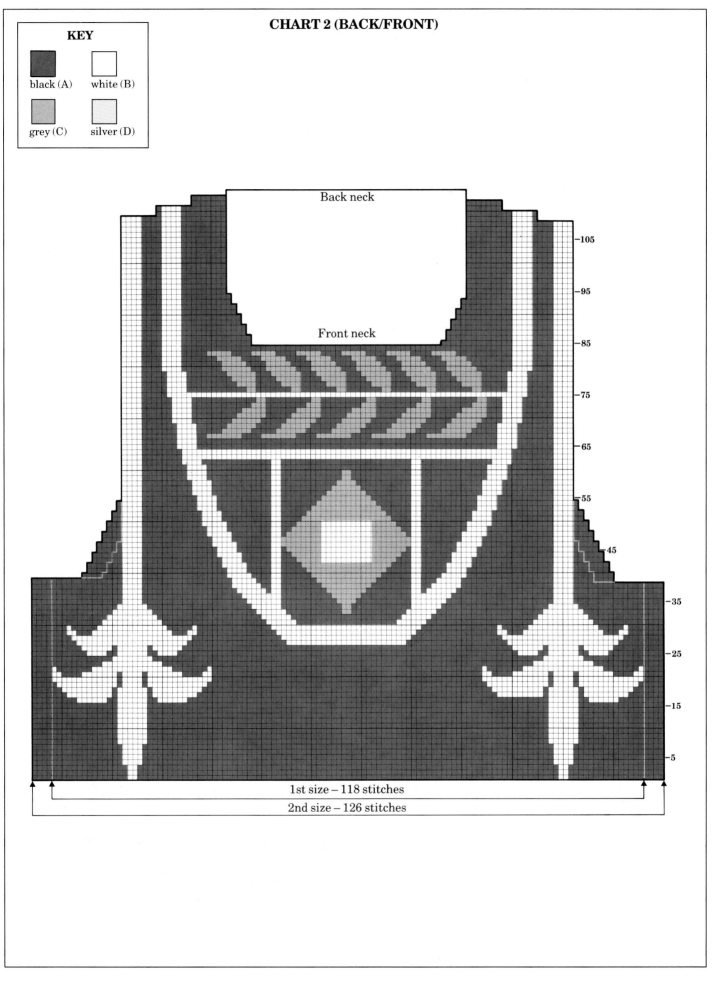

KEY

black (A) white (B)

grey (C) silver (D)

Back neck

Front neck

1st size – 118 stitches

2nd size – 126 stitches

Shape top

Keeping chart correct, cast off 10 sts at beg of next 2 rows.

Now dec 1 st at each end of next row and then every foll alt row 6 times in all.

Now dec 1 st at each end of every row 12(15) times, then dec 2 sts at each end of every row until 28(30)sts remain. Cast off.

TO MAKE UP

Sew in all ends and press pieces lightly on wrong side under a damp cloth.

DECORATION

Sew the coins, metal studs, beads and the rhinestone onto front panel (**Diagram 1**). Sew coins onto top sleeve and silver beads in middle and studs onto cuff (**Diagram 2**).

Attach studs to decorative border pattern above welt (**Diagram 3** – see page 40 for diagrams).

Neckband

Join right shoulder seam.

With 3¼mm needles and B and RS facing, pick up and K26 sts down left side of front neck, 36 sts at centre front, 26 sts at right side of front neck and 48 sts across back neck – 136 sts. Work in K1, P1 rib for 4 rows. Cast off evenly in rib.

To complete

Join left shoulder seam and neckband. Join top sleeve edges to armhole edges, easing in as necessary. Join underarm and side seams. Carefully press the garment avoiding the decorated areas.

VERSION 2

WORKED IN PURPLE, WHITE, TURQUOISE AND BROWN

MATERIALS

Yarn

Use double-knit weight: 400(450)g/15(16)oz purple (A), 150g(6oz) white (B), 25g(1oz) each turquoise (C), brown (D)

Needles and tension as for Version 1.

For decoration

1 large clear rhinestone

20 oval clear rhinestones

20 oval gold rhinestones

METHOD

Follow pattern as for Version 1 but work in colours as given above. When pieces are finished decorate as follows: front panel (**Diagram 4**); sleeve (**Diagram 5**). See page 40 for diagrams.

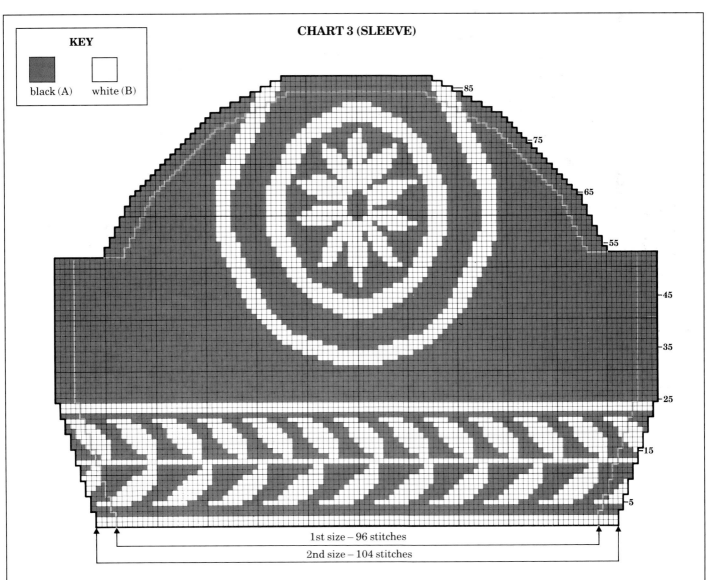

CHART 3 (SLEEVE)

KEY

black (A)   white (B)

85
75
65
55
45
35
25
15
5

1st size – 96 stitches

2nd size – 104 stitches

VERSION 3

WORKED IN TWO COLOURS ONLY WITH NO DECORATION

MATERIALS
Yarn
Use double-knit weight: 450(500)g/16(18)oz aqua (A), 50g(2oz) white (B)
Needles and tension as for Version 1.

METHOD
Work as for Version 1 but work only the border pattern on front **(Chart 1)**.
Now work in A only in st st following chart for shapings and omitting all motifs.
Work back as for Version 1.
On sleeves work cuff as for Version 1, then work rest of sleeve in A omitting all decoration.
Work neckband in B as for Version 1.

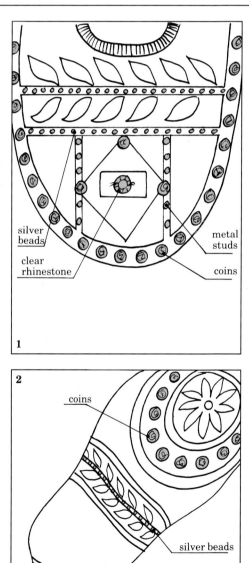

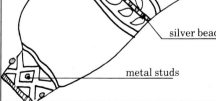

1 Version 1: decorate front panel with coins, studs, beads and the rhinestone.
2 Version 1: decorate sleeves with coins, beads and studs.

3 Version 1: studs on decorative border pattern above welt. **4** Version 2: rhinestone on centre of yoke. **5** Version 2: rhinestones on sleeve top.

opposite
Version 2: the same pattern is used but the background colour changes to purple while brown and turquoise are used on the yoke. The sleeve tops are decorated with clear and gold rhinestones; there is no decoration elsewhere except for the large rhinestone on the centre of the yoke. The sweater is worn with Version 1 of the toga which has circular motifs in white, purple, brown, grey and turquoise on a black background.

Version 3: a plain style knitted in aqua, with white used only for the border pattern and the neckband; it is shown with Version 2 of the toga which has the coloured circular motifs on a white background and bead decoration.

ROMAN TOGA

MEASUREMENTS
The finished toga/wrap measures approximately 81cm (32in) wide and 214cm (84in) long.

VERSION 1

MATERIALS
Yarn
Use double-knit weight: 575g(21oz) black (A), 125g(5oz) white (B), 75g(3oz) purple (C), 100g(4oz) brown (D), 75g(3oz) grey (E), 50g(2oz) turquoise (F)
Needles
1 pair of 4½mm (US 7) needles
1 4½mm (US 7) circular needle 100cm(39in) in length
Tension
22 sts and 26 rows to 10cm (4in) on 4½mm needles over st st.

NOTES

● Any double-knit weight yarn can be used as long as the tension is the same as that given above.

● This wrap is knitted in three separate long strips which are then sewn together.

● When working circle motifs from chart, use separate balls of yarn for each colour area worked, twisting yarns around each other on wrong side at joins to avoid holes; do not weave in at back of work unless the colours come close together – but when working leaf border patt, weave yarns in at back of work over not more than 3 sts at a time to keep fabric elastic.

METHOD
With 4½mm needles and A, cast on 60 sts and starting with a K row work 5 rows in st st.
Fold-line: (WS facing) K.
Now work from chart, starting with a K row (row 1) and work straight until row 291 has been worked (see page 44).
Now starting from row 28, work the complete chart once more (8 circle motifs worked). Work a further 2 rows in st st in A only (10 rows worked in all from last circle motif).
Now work border in reverse by turning chart upside down and working rows 27-1 in reverse order. Now with RS facing P1 row in A for fold-line. Work 5 rows in st st in A. Cast off.

Work another piece exactly the same.
Now work the third piece in the same way but work the motifs in a different order: 3rd, 4th, 1st and 2nd **(Diagram 1)**.

TO MAKE UP
Sew in all ends carefully and press pieces lightly on wrong side.
Now carefully pin the three pieces together placing the third piece in the centre and aligning the circles **(Diagram 2)**.
Tack the pieces loosely together.

1 Third piece of toga showing order of motifs. **2** Pin the three pieces of the toga together aligning the circles. **3** Turn up the hem.

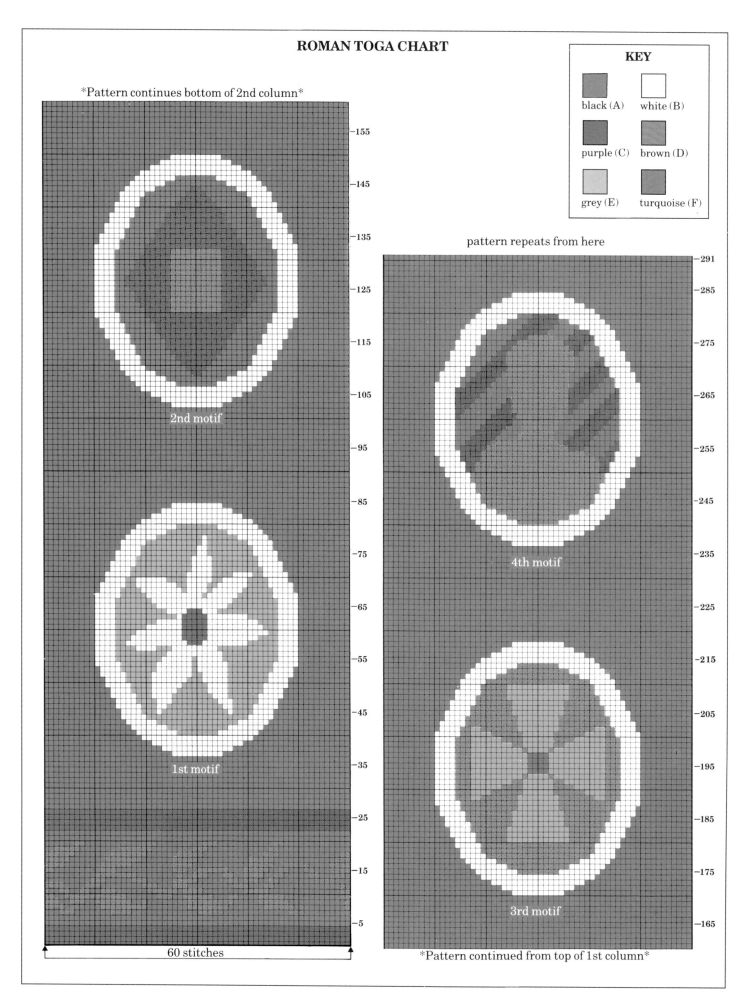

ROMAN TOGA CHART

KEY

black (A) white (B)

purple (C) brown (D)

grey (E) turquoise (F)

Pattern continues bottom of 2nd column

—155

—145

—135

—125

—115

—105

2nd motif

—95

—85

—75

—65

—55

—45

1st motif

—35

—25

—15

—5

60 stitches

pattern repeats from here

—291

—285

—275

—265

—255

—245

—235

4th motif

—225

—215

—205

—195

3rd motif

—185

—175

—165

Pattern continued from top of 1st column

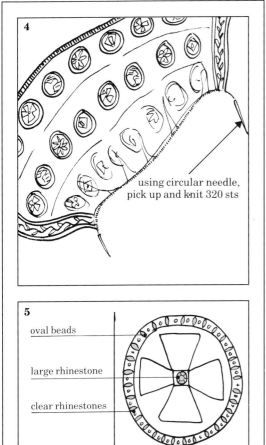

4

using circular needle, pick up and knit 320 sts

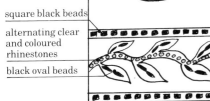

5

oval beads

large rhinestone

clear rhinestones

square black beads

alternating clear and coloured rhinestones

black oval beads

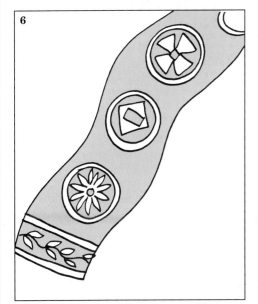

6

4 Using circular needle pick up and knit approx 320 sts along each edge of the toga. 5 Version 2: decorate the toga with beads and rhinestones as shown. 6 Version 3: the toga is knitted in two colours only – grey and white.

Now using A, carefully flat stitch the seams together. Press seams. Turn the hems onto the wrong side and slip stitch down (**Diagram 3** – see page 43).

Side edgings

Alike. Using the circular 4½mm needle and A and with RS facing, pick up and K approx 320 sts evenly along one edge of wrap and work 1 row of K1, P1 rib.

Cast off loosely in rib (**Diagram 4**).

Press completed toga/wrap carefully on wrong side paying special attention to edgings and hems at either end.

VERSION 2

This is worked exactly as for Version 1, but reverse yarns A and B so that the background is in white.

For decoration

Approx 200 assorted beads
Approx 300 black beads
Approx 200 small rhinestones in 2 colours (100 of each)
Approx 12 large rhinestones

METHOD

Decorate the toga/wrap with beads and rhinestones as shown in **Diagram 5**. Select some of the circle motifs to decorate – do not decorate them all as the beads will make the wrap too heavy.

VERSION 3

IN TWO COLOURS ONLY

MATERIALS

Yarn

Use double-knit: 750g(27oz) grey (A), 200g(8oz) white (B)
Needles and tension as for Version 1, but the toga/wrap is worked in two colours only as shown in **Diagram 6**.
Follow all other instructions as for Version 1.

BYZANTINE AND MEDIEVAL
INTRODUCTION

The two historical sweaters in this chapter are inspired by contemporary but contrasting cultures. One recalls the dress of the young nobles and merchants of medieval western Europe, men of the vigorous age of the Crusades and soaring Gothic architecture. The other echoes the costume of the much older Byzantine culture, which dominated the eastern half of the Roman Empire after the fall of Rome, and was a rich centre of culture throughout the Dark Ages.

In the fourth century AD, the Emperor Constantine moved his capital east from Rome to the Greek town of Byzantium, which came to be known as Constantinople (modern Istanbul). The city, and the empire to which it gave its name, straddled Europe and Asia. It is not surprising, particularly after western Europe was cut off by northern invasions, that Byzantine art absorbed influences from the East, mixing the classical with the more exotic.

The trend can be traced in the evolution of Byzantine costume. For most of the Byzantine period, the thousand years from 500 to 1500, a tunic based on the Roman model was the standard item of male clothing. Court dress, as depicted in mosaics and paintings, was a long tunic, with an additional length of contrasting, often very ornate, fabric draped over it – the latter a vestige of the Roman toga. For everyday wear a shorter tunic, belted at the waist, with long sleeves, was worn. Oriental influence, however, was increasingly evident in the fabric and decoration.

Many luxurious fabrics were imported to Constantinople from the East – brocades and damasks from Persia and Arabia, silk from China – as well as cotton and linen from Egypt. Such was the demand for these materials that a local textile industry arose. Silkworms were introduced via Persia during the reign of the Emperor Justinian (527-561); palace and private silk works were set up, although by law the finest quality brocades could be produced only on the palace looms. The fabrics were woven in lively designs in gorgeous colours often in bold blocks, and sometimes pure gold thread was used for extra sumptuousness. Motifs included geometric shapes, swirling spirals and ovals, and representational figures – extant fragments of fine silk even show stylized eagles and elephants. Often garments were made up from panels of different fabrics, some plain, some elaborately patterned or embroidered.

The Byzantine Sweater (see photograph, page 49) is inspired by the rich pattern and colour of these fabrics; the scrollwork motif in the decorative panel and on the cuffs and the rectangles overlaid with contrasting colours are both seen on clothing of the period. There are other characteristic features: the single vertical black band, right of centre on the front, is derived from the Roman *clavi*, the name given to a pair of such bands used to ornament the Roman tunic, which were retained on dress throughout the Byzantine period; the asymmetrical decorative panel itself recalls

Detail from a Byzantine mosaic at Ravenna shows the Empress Theodora, wife of Justinian, wearing a magnificent jewelled crown and collar.

the ornate insignia worn by high dignitaries on the front of their cloaks; and the pattern of interlocking black and red rectangles on the panel and right sleeve is inspired, not by fabric design, but by mosaics, an art at which the Byzantines excelled.

The rhinestones, 'jet' beads and golden studs on the sweater give a truly Byzantine flavour. Like Byzantine metal-work, the clothing was often encrusted with all kinds of gems – even diamonds and pearls. Sometimes pieces of mirror glass were added – a device still used today in the East. It is ironic, however, that in the fifteenth century, the impoverishment of the Empire in its last days was such that the Imperial jewels are known to have been made from coloured glass: even a twentieth-century sweater can rival Byzantine emperors in splendour!

The Medieval Sweater (see photograph, page 59), like the Byzantine, imitates the tunics of the day, which are also thought to have derived from Roman dress. The basic garment went through various changes in the medieval period: first loose and belted at the waist, then becoming shorter with a belt worn low over the hips, finally evolving into the fifteenth-century doublet, padded at the front and with full sleeves. Sue Bradley's sweater is modelled on this last style.

Like the Byzantines, the people of medieval Europe loved the glowing colours seen in illuminated manuscripts, in painting and, most memorably perhaps, in stained glass. All classes of society wore bright colours when they could; even the peasants' coarse homespun tunics could be dyed bright green, blue or even red. A vogue for parti-coloured clothes from the twelfth century onwards made much use of contrasting stripes, chequers and diamonds. Asymmetrical patterning was also popular – it is subtly incorporated into the design of this sweater, where the colour order is reversed on the sleeves.

In the late Middle Ages especially, gold embroidery and gems were applied to ornament clothing further. The beading and gold studs on the Medieval Sweater reflect this taste, and the deep beaded welt imitates the heavily embroidered jewel-studded or metal-mesh belts worn by both sexes.

Accessories for both the Byzantine and Medieval sweaters are included: the leggings are based on hose, the universal legwear worn with tunics. They are patterned in black and white in a typical medieval diaper design of diamonds containing a geometric motif.

The earrings are primarily Byzantine, imitating beaten gold with a large gemstone simply set, while the headband recalls both the tiaras of Byzantine princesses and the gold circlet used by medieval ladies to hold a veil in place.

The hood belongs in the colder climate of northern Europe. It is taken partly from the *couvrechef,* a loose fabric head-covering worn by women in the early Middle Ages, and partly from the *liripipe,* a hood with a long tail that was standard attire for men from the thirteenth century onwards. The marabou feathers on the white knitted background imitate ermine, a highly valued fur worn by medieval nobles as a trimming or lining to their clothes and today an emblem of royalty. For most people in the fourteenth century an ermine *liripipe* would have been an unimaginable and possibly impractical luxury; today's knitted imitation is considerably cheaper and easier to wear.

Illustration from the Roman de la Rose *(c. 1487-95) which shows clearly the bright colours of medieval dress: reds, blues, greens and yellow.*

BYZANTINE SWEATER

MEASUREMENTS (see also page 168)

Three sizes	small	medium	large
To fit bust: Actual measurement: Length from shoulder: Sleeve seam:	81-86cm (32-34in) 102cm (40¼in) 69cm (27in) 46cm (18in)	91-97cm (36-38in) 108cm (42½in) 69cm (27in) 48cm (19in)	102-107cm (40-42in) 114cm (45in) 69cm (27in) 50cm (20in)

VERSION 1

MATERIALS
Yarn
Use Aran weight: 225(250 : 275)g/8(9 : 10)oz blue wool (A), 175(200)g/7(8)oz black wool (B), 100(125)g/4(5)oz red wool (C), 50(75)g/2(3)oz gold lurex – use 3 strands together (D), 25g(1oz) green cotton (E), 50(75)g/2(3)oz white viscose (F)

Needles and other materials
1 pair each of 4½mm (US 7) and 5½mm (US 9) needles
Spare needle
Shirring elastic
Darning needle

For decoration
73 black drop beads
26 gold clip-on metal studs
50 small sew-on rhinestones in assorted colours
9 large assorted sew-on rhinestones
14 medium green sew-on rhinestones
9 medium blue sew-on rhinestones
4 medium red sew-on rhinestones

Tension
18 sts and 22 rows to 10cm (4in) on 5½mm needles over st st using Aran yarn.
20 sts and 22 rows to 10cm (4in) on 5½mm needles over Fair Isle pattern.

NOTES

- Any Aran-weight yarn can be used, as long as the tension is the same as that given above.

- When working from charts, strand yarn loosely across wrong side of work over not more than 3 sts at a time to keep fabric elastic. When working centre stripe, use separate balls of yarn, and twist yarns around each other on wrong side at joins to avoid a hole.

FRONT
With 5½mm needles and A, cast on 92(98 : 104)sts and starting with a K row, work 2 rows in st st.
Next row: (RS facing) P in A for fold-line.
Next row: P in A.
Now cont in st st and place stripe as follows:
Next row: (RS facing) K50(53 : 56)A, 12B, 30 (33 : 36)A.
Next row: P30(33 : 36)A, 12B, 50(53 : 56)A.
These 2 rows place the centre stripe and are repeated. On next row, keeping centre stripe correct, fold hem by picking up all the 92(98 : 104)

sts along cast-on edge on a spare needle. Fold up hem, and holding spare needle behind left-hand needle, knit together one stitch from each of the needles across row (**Diagram 1**).
Now cont straight in st st with centre stripe patt until front measures 32cm (12½in) from fold-line, ending with a WS row.
Now place **Chart 1** (see page 50) as follows:
Next row: K14(17 : 20)A, now work across the 78(81 : 84)sts on row 1 of chart.
This row places the chart.
Cont to follow chart until row 64 has been worked reading K rows (odd-numbered rows) from right to left and P rows (even-numbered rows) from left to right.

Shape front neck
Next row: (row 65, RS facing) Patt 39(42 : 45)sts, cast off centre 14 sts, patt to end, and cont on this last set of sts only.
** Keeping chart correct, dec 1 st at neck edge on next 10 rows – 29(32 : 35)sts.
Now cont straight following chart until row 79 has been worked.

Shape shoulder
Keeping chart correct, cast off 7(8 : 9)sts at beg of next row (row 80) and foll 2 alt rows.
Patt 1 row.
Cast off rem 8 sts.
With WS facing, rejoin yarn to rem sts and work as for first side from ** to end, noting that shoulder shaping starts on row 79.

BACK
Cast on and work as for front, but omitting the centre B stripe.
Cont straight in st st and A only until back measures 38cm (15in) from fold-line, ending with a WS row.

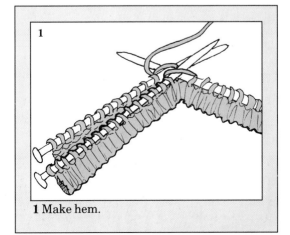

1 Make hem.

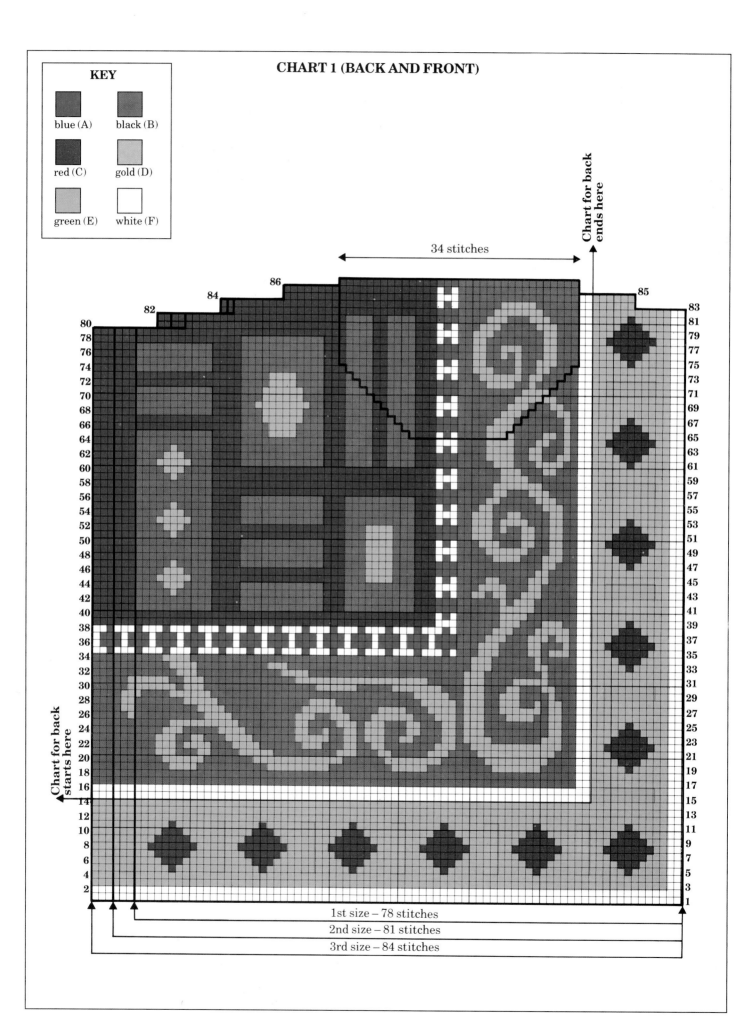

CHART 1 (BACK AND FRONT)

KEY

blue (A) black (B)

red (C) gold (D)

green (E) white (F)

34 stitches

Chart for back ends here

Chart for back starts here

1st size – 78 stitches
2nd size – 81 stitches
3rd size – 84 stitches

Now place **Chart 1** as follows (noting that chart for back starts on row 15 and is only 65(68 : 71)sts wide and is a mirror image of chart for front): This is worked by reading K rows (odd-numbered rows) from left to right, and P rows (even-numbered rows) from right to left.
Row 1 is placed as follows:
K across the 65(68 : 71)sts, reading from left to right, of row 15 of chart, then K 27(30 : 33)A.
Row 2: P27(30 : 33)A, then P65(68 : 71)sts of row 16 of chart, reading right to left. Cont straight in st st and follow chart as now set until row 78 has been worked (omit all front neck shapings).

Shape shoulders
(Start on row 79.) Keeping chart correct, cast off 7(8 : 9)sts at beg of next 6 rows, and 8 sts at beg of foll 2 rows. Cast off rem 34 sts for back neck.

RIGHT SLEEVE
Decorative cuff
With 4½mm needles and F, cast on 36 sts and work in K1, P1 rib for 1 row. With F, P 1 row.

> **NOTE**
> • Tension differs on this sleeve due to Fair Isle pattern.

Change to 5½mm needles and work from **Chart 2,** reading K rows (odd-numbered rows) from right to left and P rows (even-numbered rows) from left to right. Work over the 36 sts as set until row 14 of chart has been worked. Change to 4½mm needles.
Next row: (RS facing) with F, K 1 row.
Work in K1, P1 rib in F for 2 rows ***.
Change to 5½mm needles and P 1 row in C.
Increase row: (RS facing) K in C, and inc 24 sts evenly across row – 60 sts.
Now work from **Chart 3** (see page 52) as follows:
On K rows (odd-numbered rows) reading from right to left, and P rows (even-numbered rows) reading from left to right, inc 1 st at each end of 4th row and then every foll 4th row as shown until there are 100 sts on the needle.
Cast off on row 81(85 : 91) as indicated on chart.

LEFT SLEEVE
Cast on and work decorative cuff as for right sleeve to ***.
Change to 5½mm needles and P 1 row in A.
Increase row: (RS facing) K in A, and inc 24 sts evenly across row – 60 sts.
Now work in st st in A only, and inc 1 st at each end of 4th row and then every foll 4th row (as for right sleeve) but working until there are 90 sts only on needle.
(Less sts are due to the different tensions used on sleeves.) Cont straight in st st on these sts until sleeve measures the same as right sleeve, ending with a WS row. Cast off all sts.

TO MAKE UP
Sew in all ends and carefully press pieces according to ball band instructions on wrong side, paying special attention to Fair Isle panels. Join left shoulder seam.

Neckband
With 4½mm needles and B and with RS facing, pick up and K 30 sts across back neck, 20 sts down left side neck, 12 sts across centre front

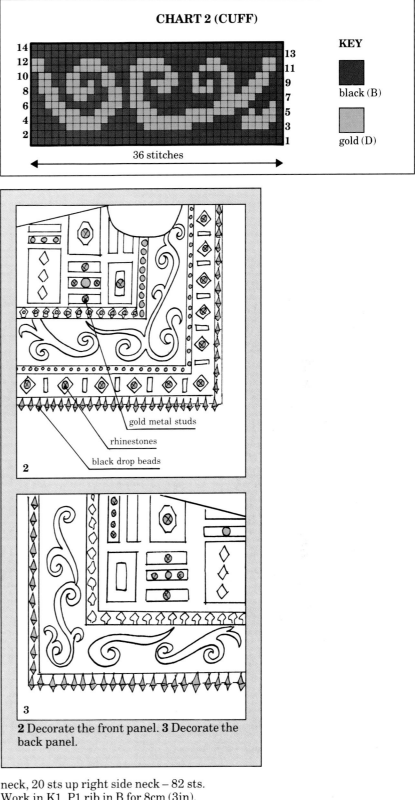

CHART 2 (CUFF)

14 · 12 · 10 · 8 · 6 · 4 · 2 — 13 · 11 · 9 · 7 · 5 · 3 · 1

36 stitches

KEY

black (B)

gold (D)

gold metal studs
rhinestones
black drop beads

2

3

2 Decorate the front panel. **3** Decorate the back panel.

neck, 20 sts up right side neck – 82 sts.
Work in K1, P1 rib in B for 8cm (3in).
Work 2 rows in rib in D.
With a 5½mm needle, cast off loosely in rib in D.
Join right shoulder and neckband seam.

To complete
Decorate front panel **(Diagram 2).** Decorate back panel **(Diagram 3).** Decorate right sleeve **(Diagram 4** see page 53**).**
With centre of cast-off edges of sleeves to shoulder seams, position sleeves, reaching down to same patt band on back and front. Sew in position. Join side, sleeve and cuff seams.

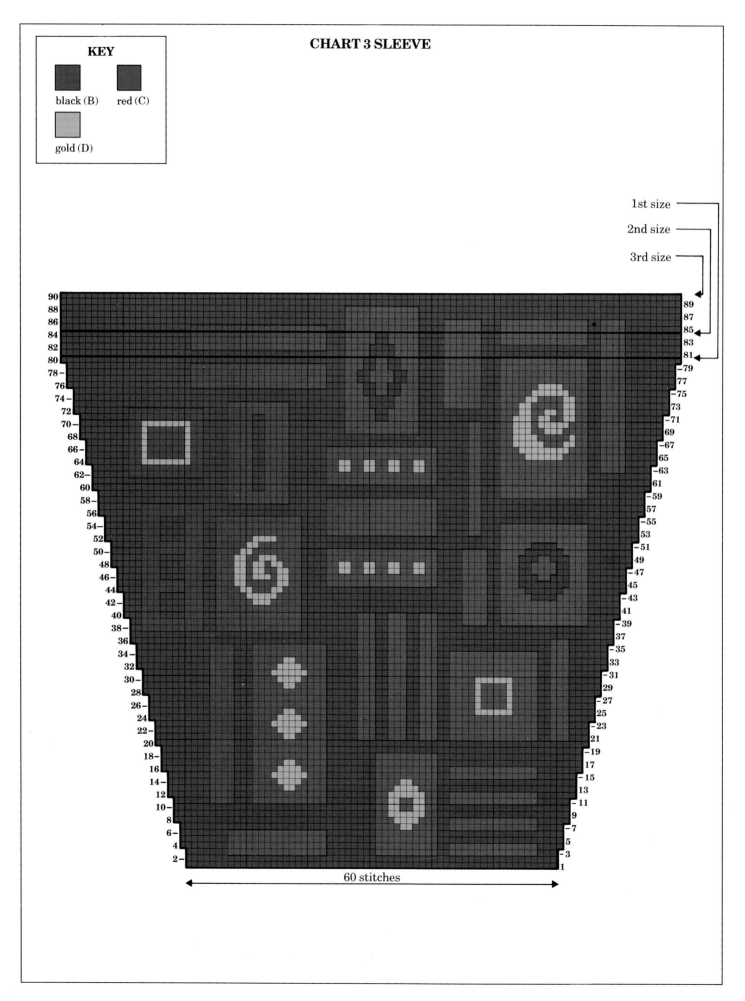

CHART 3 SLEEVE

KEY

black (B)   red (C)

gold (D)

1st size

2nd size

3rd size

60 stitches

To insert elastic
(If you cannot find the correct shade of elastic, buy a permanent felt-tip pen in the matching shade and colour the elastic.)
Start 15cm (6in) up from the fold-line of the back and, using a large darning needle, thread the elastic in and out of the sts on the wrong side **(Diagram 5)**. Rep until the elastic is threaded through the whole waist. Adjust to fit and fasten off securely. If required a couple of rows of elastic can be inserted. Run some elastic through edges of cuffs as for waist. Fold neckband in half to the right side and carefully stitch down.

VERSION 2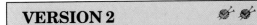

SWEATER WITH PLAIN SLEEVES, CUFFS AND BACK

MATERIALS
Yarn
Use Aran weight: 100(125 : 150)g/4(5 : 6)oz blue wool (A), 75(100 : 125)g/3(4 : 5)oz black wool (B), 425(450 : 475)g/15(16 : 17)oz red wool (C), 50g(2oz) gold lurex – use 3 strands together (D), 25g(1oz) green cotton (E), 50g(2oz) white viscose (F)
Needles and tension as for Version 1.

METHOD
The main background colour is changed by substituting yarn C for A and yarn A for C.

FRONT
With 5½mm needles and C, cast on 92 (98 : 104) sts and work fold-line as for Version 1. Cont to work as for Version 1, but omit the vertical black stripe and instead cont straight in C in st st until front measures 32cm (12½in) from cast-on edge, ending with a WS row. Now work from **Chart 1**, as for Version 1, still substituting C for A.

BACK
Work as for Version 1 but work in C only omitting all motifs.

SLEEVES
Make 2. With 4½mm needles and C, cast on 36 sts and work in K1, P1 rib for 9cm (3½in).
Increase row: Rib and inc 24 sts evenly across row – 60 sts. Change to 5½mm needles and starting with a K row work in st st in C only and inc 1 st at each end of every foll 4th row (as on **Chart 3**) until there are 90 sts on the needle. Cont straight until sleeve measures 46 (48 : 50)cm/18(19 : 20)in from cast-on edge ending with a WS row. Cast off loosely in C.
Follow all making up instructions as for Version 1, but omit the decoration.

VERSION 3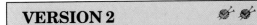

SWEATER WITH THREE SIMPLE COLOUR BLOCKS

MATERIALS
Yarn
Use Aran weight: 50g(2oz) blue wool (A), 525(550 : 575)g/19(20 : 21)oz black wool (B), 50g(2oz) each red wool (C), green cotton (E), 25g(1oz) white viscose (F)
Needles and tension as for Version 1.

FRONT
Work as for Version 1, but reverse yarns by substituting yarn A for B and yarn B for A.
Follow chart to row 3.
Now work as follows:
Rows 3-14: Work from chart, but instead of working red diamonds and green stripes work the whole section in green (E); cont to work from chart so that the now plain horizontal band in E continues into the vertical band.
Rows 15 and 16: As Version 1.
Rows 17-34: Omit scroll patt in D and work this section in red (C).
Rows 35-38: Omit small diamonds and work this this section in white (F).
Cont these plain bands vertically and work rows 39 to end of chart in plain bands with blue (A) on right-hand side of front.

BACK AND SLEEVES
(Both worked in black).
Follow instructions as for Version 2, but using yarn B.

TO MAKE UP
Follow making up instructions for Version 1 but omit the decoration.
Neckband is worked in yarn B omitting gold stripe.

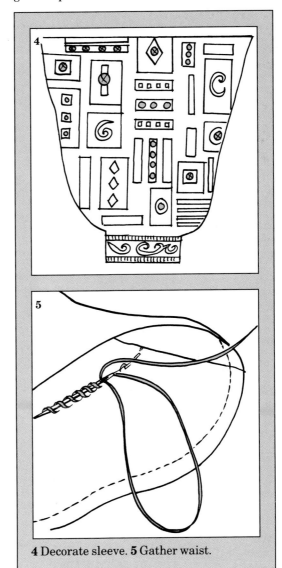

4 Decorate sleeve. **5** Gather waist.

Version 2: a simpler undecorated sweater with plain sleeves.

*Version 3: the same basic pattern is transformed into a contemporary-looking sweater
decorated with asymmetrical blocks of colour.*

ACCESSORIES

EARRINGS

MATERIALS
Yarn
Small amount of gold lurex worked double
Needles
1 pair of 4mm (US 6) needles
For decoration
2 large coloured rhinestones
6 black drop beads
Cardboard
Earring fitments

METHOD
With 4mm needles and yarn double, cast on 8 sts
and starting with a K row, work 24 rows in st st.
Cast off. Work another piece the same.

TO COMPLETE
Cut out two squares of thin cardboard approx
4cm (1½in) square.
Fold one oblong of knitting in half, sandwich one
cardboard square in the middle and stitch the
knitting carefully together around the edges of
the cardboard **(Diagram 1)**.
Sew a large rhinestone to centre of square and
stitch drop beads onto three corners of square.
Attach earring fitment to the remaining corner
(Diagram 2).
Cover second square in the same way.

HOOD

MATERIALS
Yarn
Use double-knit wool: 200g(8oz) white (A),
25g(1oz) gold lurex worked double (B)
Needles
1 pair of 4mm (US 6) needles
For decoration
A strip of black marabou feathers approx 1 metre
in length or a bag of 30 black marabou feathers

Tension
28 sts and 28 rows to 10cm (4in) on 4mm needles
over rib (without stretching).

METHOD
With 4mm needles and B, cast on 140 sts and
work in K1, P1, rib for 4 rows. Change to A and
cont in rib as set until work measures 46cm
(18in) from cast-on edge.
Next row: *K1, (K1, P1 into next st), rep from *
to end – 210 sts.
Now cont in rib as follows:
Row 1: (WS facing) *K2, P1, rep from * to end.
Row 2: *K1, P2, rep from * to end.
Cont to rep the last 2 rib rows until work
measures 63.5cm (25in) from cast-on edge,
ending with a WS row.
Now work 4 rows of K1, P1, rib in B.
Cast off very loosely in rib in B.

TO COMPLETE
Join centre back seam.

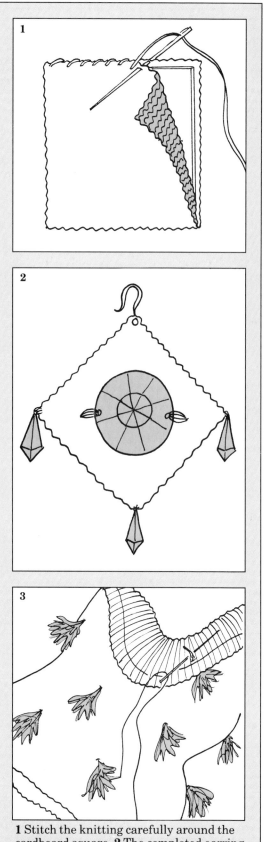

1 Stitch the knitting carefully around the
cardboard square. **2** The completed earring.
3 Stitch down feathers at back of hood.

DECORATION

The hood can be left plain, decorated with beads and stones, or as in the example shown, tufted with marabou feathers to give the effect of ermine. Cut the feathers into small sections about 2.5cm (1in) long.
Stitch onto hood. Push ends of feathers through to the back of work and stitch down neatly **(Diagram 3).**

Medieval hood knitted in white double-knit wool ribbing trimmed with gold lurex and black marabou feathers.

HEADBAND

MATERIALS
Yarn
Small amount each gold lurex, use 3 strands together (A), red Aran wool (B), blue Aran wool (C)
Needles
1 pair of 5½mm (US 9) needles
For decoration
Approx 15 gold beads

METHOD
With 5½mm needles and A, cast on 12 sts, and starting with a K row, work in st st in the following stripe sequence:
6 rows in A. 2 rows in B.
6 rows in A. 2 rows in C.
These 16 rows form the stripe sequence and are repeated as required.
Cont straight as set until band is correct length to fit around head, when slightly stretched.
Cast off.

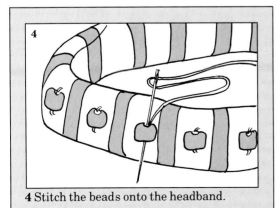

4 Stitch the beads onto the headband.

TO MAKE UP

Decorate band with gold beads **(Diagram 4).**
Sew cast-on and cast-off edges together.
Join long edge together, stitching carefully and invisibly on outside with gold thread.

LEGGINGS

MEASUREMENTS
Total length approx: 71cm (28in)
Total width approx: 41cm (16in)

MATERIALS
Yarn
Use double-knit weight: 200g(8oz) white (A), 100g(4oz) black (B)
Needles
1 pair each of 3¼mm (US 3) and 4mm (US 6) needles

Tension
24 sts and 26 rows to 10cm (4in) on 4mm needles over Fair Isle pattern.

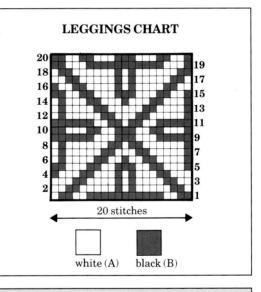

LEGGINGS CHART

20 stitches

white (A)   black (B)

NOTE

- Any double knit-weight yarn can be used, as long as the tension is the same as that given.

TO MAKE
Make 2. With 3¼mm needles and A, cast on 66 sts and work in K1, P1 rib for 7.5cm (3in).
Increase row: Rib and inc 34 sts evenly across row – 100 sts.
Change to 4mm needles and work in st st and pattern from chart as follows:
Work the 20 stitch patt repeat 5 times across row.
Cont to follow chart until row 20 has been worked, then repeat the 20 row patt until work measures approx 56cm (22in) from cast-on edge, ending with a 10th or 20th patt row.
Next row: (RS facing) K in A.
Change to 3¼mm needles and work in K1, P1 rib for 15cm (6in).
Cast off fairly loosely in rib using a 4mm needle.

To complete
Join centre back seam matching pattern carefully.

MEDIEVAL SWEATER

MEASUREMENTS (see also page 168)

Three sizes	small	medium	large
To fit bust:	81-86cm(32-34in)	91-97cm(36-38in)	102-107cm(40-42in)
Actual measurement:	105cm(41½in)	112cm(44in)	120cm(47¼in)
Length from shoulder:	61cm(24in)	63cm(24¾in)	66cm(26in)
Sleeve seam:	51cm(20in)	51cm(20in)	51cm(20in)

VERSION 1

MATERIALS
Yarn
Use Aran wool and mohair: 150(175 : 200)g/
6(7 : 8)oz black Aran wool (A), 100(125 : 150)g/
4(5 : 6)oz blue mohair (B), 100(125 : 150)g/
4(5 : 6)oz green mohair (C), 100g(4oz) red mohair
(D), 50(50 : 75)g/2(2 : 3)oz gold lurex - use 3
strands together (E)
Needles
1 pair each of 5mm (US 8) and 6mm
(US 10) needles
For decoration
Approx 250 gold clip-on metal studs
Approx 60 sew-on clear lozenge-shaped
rhinestones
Approx 30 each of red, blue, green and yellow
sew-on rhinestones

Tension
16 sts and 22 rows to 10cm(4in) on 6mm needles
over st st using mohair yarn.

NOTES
● Any Aran weight and mohair can be
used, as long as the tension is the same as
that given.

● Use separate balls of yarn for each colour
area worked, twisting yarns around each
other on wrong side at joins to avoid holes.

BACK
With 5mm needles and E, cast on 66(72 : 78)sts
and work 3 rows of K1, P1, rib. Break off E.
Change to A and work a further 22 rows in rib as
set. Break off A.
Change to E and work a further 3 rows in rib.**
Increase row: Rib in E and inc 18 sts evenly
across row – 84(90 : 96)sts.
Change to 6mm needles and work in st st and
place pattern as follows:
Row 1: (RS facing) *K11(12 : 13)C, K3D, K11(12 :
13)B, K3D, rep from * to end.
Row 2: *P3D, P11(12 : 13)B, P3D, P11(12 : 13)C,
rep from * to end. These 2 rows make up the
pattern for the front and back.
Cont straight in patt as set until back measures
44(46 : 49)cm/17¼(18 : 19¼)in from cast-on edge,
ending with a WS row. Break off all contrast
colours.

Yoke
With E, K1 row.
Change to 5mm needles and work 3 rows in
single rib, as for welt, in E.

Break off E and join in A.
Cont in rib as set in A until back measures 61(63 :
66)cm/24(24¾ : 26)in from cast-on edge, ending
with a WS row.

Shape shoulders
Keeping rib correct, cast off 7(8 : 9)sts at beg of
next 6 rows.
Cont on rem 42 sts for collar in A as follows:
Increase row: K1, (K1, P1 into next st), rep from
* to end – 63sts.
Next row: (WS facing) P1, *K1, P1, rep from
* to end.
Next row: K1, *P1, K1, rep from * to end.
Rep these 2 rows until collar measures 10cm
(4in). Break off A.
Join in E and work a further 3 rows in rib.
Cast off loosely in rib using a 6mm needle.

FRONT
Work exactly the same as for back.

RIGHT SLEEVE
With 5mm needles and E, cast on 32 sts and work
in rib as for back welt to **.
Increase row Rib in E, inc 1 st in every st across
row – 64 sts.
Change to 6mm needles and work in st st and
stripe pattern as follows, at the same time, inc 1
st at each end of 2nd row and then every foll 3rd
row until 112 sts are on the needle, then cont
straight until stripe sequence is complete.
Stripe sequence
Work 16 rows in st st in C; 4 rows in st st in D; 16
rows in st st in B; 4 rows in st st in D; 16 rows in
st st in C; 4 rows in st st in D; 16 rows in st st in B;
4 rows in st st in D (80 rows in all).
Cast off loosely in D.

LEFT SLEEVE
Work as for right sleeve but reverse the position
of yarns B and C so that you start with a blue
stripe and end with a green stripe.

TO MAKE UP
Carefully join shoulder seams and side collar
edge together. Run a gathering thread through
the tops of the sleeves and gather up to 51cm(20in)
with the majority of the gathers over the centre
top of sleeve so that they will puff over the
shoulder. Carefully sew in sleeves to armhole
edges, placing centre of cast-off edges of sleeves to
shoulder seams. Remove the gathering thread.
Join underarm and side seams matching stripes
and sewing each stripe up in matching yarn. Fold
collar to right side and stitch down lightly on
either side of neck to hold in place.
Pattern continued on page 164.

*opposite
Version 1: medieval sweater
knitted in glowing stripes
with mohair and Aran
wool. The body and sleeves
are decorated with gold
studs and the yoke and welt
are embellished with
rhinestones.*

Version 2: the sweater is striped in green, blue and black only. Yoke, cuffs and welt are trimmed in gold but have no decoration.

Version 3: the body and sleeves are knitted in plain blue mohair with yoke, cuffs and welt in black Aran wool.

RENAISSANCE
INTRODUCTION

High Renaissance and sixteenth-century fashion is best typified by the great monarchs of the time: François I and Henry VIII, resplendent in doublets and capes, or Elizabeth I, elaborately ruffed and bejewelled. Indeed it was at their courts, and at those of other European potentates that ostentation in dress reached its height, since the power of a courtier could be measured by the magnificence of his personal adornment.

Elizabethan dress as shown on a late sixteenth-century embroidery.

Those who could afford to, wore expensive figured silks and brocades from the Orient, velvets and brocaded gold cloth from Venice, heavy silks and satins from Bruges – all profusely embroidered with silk, gold or silver thread and even gems. Both the designs in this chapter reflect this taste for lavish decoration in their use of eye-catching gold lurex yarn and, on the black and gold sweater, of pearl beads.

The shape of clothes changed markedly in this period; instead of the narrow, shapeless silhouette of medieval dress, styles became wider at the shoulders and below the waist, but with a more tightly fitting bodice. (The new 'look' had originated in fifteenth-century Italy and spread throughout Europe, becoming more exaggerated as it travelled.) Typical male dress was a square-shouldered doublet or tunic, stiffened and padded over the torso and tight at the waist, worn with puffed trunk hose or short breeches and a short gown or cape.

The Renaissance Sweater I (see photograph, page 65) is modelled on the shape of the doublet, whereas Sweater II (see photograph, page 73) is inspired by women's dress, with narrower shoulders, fitted bodice and full sleeves. Women's gowns had voluminous skirts which were worn over farthingales (frames of whalebone or wire), which increased their width to give a kind of crinoline effect.

But it was the upper body that received the greatest emphasis, with padded and puffed sleeves, and doublets and bodices embroidered over every inch, shimmering with jewels and trimmed with fur or lace. Lace, produced in Italy and Flanders from about the middle of the sixteenth century, soon became enormously popular and was used with great extravagance.

The other major innovation was slashing – cutting the fabric to reveal contrasting fabrics and colours beneath, a fashion which is said to have emerged after the Battle of Grandson in 1476, when Swiss soldiers, having routed the Burgundians, plundered their camps and used costly banners and furnishings to patch their ragged uniforms. The fashion was taken up by wandering German mercenaries and became the rage throughout Europe. At its peak, in the 1520s and 30s, almost every item of clothing including shoes and hats was slashed.

The 'doublet' sweater (Sweater I) recalls this fashion, with its glowing bobbles in blue and red mohair and gold lurex. Sweater II also features a slashed effect, with its puffy bands of black and gold net also emphasizing the importance of lace as a trimming.

The colours of the period showed the same flamboyance: reds were the most popular, particularly scarlets and rich burgundies, as well as other strong hues such as emerald green, cobalt blue and bright golden yellow. But in the second half of the century a more sombre note was introduced, the result of the growing power of Spain and the sober taste of Emperor Charles V. After Philip II's succession in 1556 the Spanish court became the model for the rest of Europe and the gorgeous colours of the earlier period gave way to black. However, the austerity of the Spanish style could be modified by using the rich black of silk and velvet to offset the sparkle of jewels and the bright silks and taffetas of undershirts and skirts. The effectiveness of this contrast is illustrated in the portrait of Queen Elizabeth shown here. She wears a magnificent black, gold-embroidered dress encrusted with pearls, a style which provides the inspiration for the rich trimming of the black and gold evening Sweater II.

The ruff, so characteristic of Elizabethan dress, was also a Spanish innovation. It evolved from the soft ruffled collars popular in the early part of the century and grew to enormous proportions – the cartwheel ruff of the 1580s was 23cm (9in) wide, starched and supported on wire. For women it was often split in front to reveal the décolletage and rose behind the head like a gauzy halo. Forcing the wearer to hold the head high and relatively immobile, the ruff expressed

This portrait of Queen Elizabeth I (c. 1575) is attributed to Nicholas Hilliard. The Queen wears a black gown embroidered with a gold trellis and leaf design and encrusted with pearls. 'Slashing' and lace are also used to trim this splendid dress.

the hauteur of the courtly styles of the later Renaissance. The black and gold evening Sweater II has a high, ruffled net collar to complete the Elizabethan look, whereas the bobble Sweater I has a narrower collar edged in gold lurex to match the cuffs, in keeping with the rather more sober style of masculine dress.

Both men and women wore a variety of berets, caps, toques and hoods in the sixteenth century. To complement the bobble sweater instructions are given for making a matching cap, which, like the sweater, is studded with tiny coloured rhinestones, adding a subtle sparkle to an outfit a Renaissance courtier would have been proud to wear.

RENAISSANCE SWEATER I

MEASUREMENTS (see also page 168)

Two sizes	small-medium	medium-large
To fit bust:	81-91cm (32-36in)	91-97 (26-38in)
Actual measurement:	104cm (41in)	108cm (42½in)
Length from back neck (approx):	63cm (25in)	63cm (25in)
Sleeve seam including cuff edgings (approx):	44cm (17½in)	44cm (17½in)

VERSION 1

MATERIALS
Yarns
Use Aran weight: 300(325)g/11(12)oz black wool (A), 100g(4oz) green wool (B), 150g(6oz) red mohair (C), 100g(4oz) gold lurex worked double (D), 150g(6oz) blue mohair (E)

Needles and other materials
1 pair each of 4½mm (US 7) and 3¼mm (US 3) needles
Set of four 4½mm (US 7) needles
2 buttons
Crochet hook
Embroidery needle

For decoration
70 each of small red, blue, white and green clip-on rhinestones.
Lengths of double-knit wool in 5 colours (use the same double-knit wool and lurex as on garment, and substitute 2 toning double-knit wools for the mohair) for cording.

Tension
20 sts and 24 rows to 10cm (4in) on 3¼mm needles over main pattern.

> **NOTES**
>
> ● Any Aran weight yarn can be used, as long as the tension is the same as that given.
>
> ● When working in more than one colour, strand yard not in use loosely across wrong side of work over not more than 3 sts at a time to keep fabric elastic.

opposite
Version 1: sweater inspired by the Elizabethan doublet has a fitted body with high collar and slightly puffed sleeves. It is knitted in a bobble stitch in red and blue mohair and gold lurex on a black ground. The front panel in green, black and gold is edged with a cording which is also used around the shoulder seams to complete the rich effect. The sweater is worn with a matching skull-cap.

BACK
With 4½mm needles and A, cast on 104(108)sts and work in bobble and stripe pattern as follows:
Row 1: (RS facing) *K3A, K1B, rep from * to end.
Row 2: *P1B, P3A, rep from * to end.
Rows 3 and 4: Rep 1st and 2nd rows once more.
Rows 5: *K3A, in C (K1, P1, K1, P1) into next st, rep from * to end.
Row 6: *In C (K1, yon) 3 times and K1 over the 4 bobble sts, P3A, rep from * to end.
Row 7: *K3A, K4C (dropping yon sts), rep from * to end.
Row 8: *K4C, P3A, rep from * to end.
Row 9: *K3A, in C K2 tog twice, rep from * to end.
Row 10: *In C K2 tog, P3A, rep from * to end.
Row 11: *K3A, K1B, rep from * to end.
Row 12: *P1B, P3A, rep from * to end.

These 12 rows from the basic pattern. Work the 12 rows once more working bobbles in D.
Then rep them once more working bobbles in E (36 patt rows worked).

Shape waist
Decrease row: (RS facing) *K3 togA, K1B, rep from * to end – 52(54)sts.
Next row: *P1B, P1A, rep from * to end.
Next row: *K1A, K1B, rep from * to end.
Rep last 2 rows 3 times more then rep 1st row again.
Increase row: (RS facing) *In A (K1, P1, K1) into next st, K1B, rep from * to end – 104(108)sts.
2nd row: *P1B, P3A, rep from * to end.
Now work in the 12-row bobble and stripe pattern, starting with row 5, making bobbles in C, and cont making bobbles in colour sequence as now set, until a further 3 sets of bobbles have been worked, ending with a 12th patt row (bobbles in E have just been worked).

Shape armholes
Keeping patt correct, cast off 10 sts at beg of next 2 rows – 84(88)sts.
Now dec 1 st at beg of next 4 rows – 80(84)sts.
Cont straight in patt as set until 10 rows of bobbles have been worked, ending with a 12th patt row (bobbles in C have just been worked).

Shape shoulders
Keeping patt correct, cast off 7(8)sts at beg of next 6 rows.
Cast off rem 38(36)sts for back neck.

FRONT
With 4½mm needles and A, cast on 104(108)sts and work in bobble and stripe pattern as follows:
(NB when working in patt *do not* strand yarns C, D and E across centre panel.)
Row 1: (RS facing) *K3A, K1B, rep from * to end.
Row 2: *P1B, P3A, rep from * to end.
Rows 3 and 4: Rep 1st and 2nd rows once more.
Row 5: *K3A, in C (K1, P1, K1, P1) into next st*, rep from * to * 9 times, (K3A, K1B) 8(9) times, now rep from * to * 9 more times.
Cont in patt as now set, working centre 32(36)sts in A and B stripes only as shown.
Follow shaping exactly as for back until front measures 51cm (20in) from cast-on edge, ending with a WS row.

Shape front neck
Next row: Patt 24(26)sts, cast off centre 32 sts, and patt to end of row and cont on this last set of 24(26)sts only for first side.
Keeping patt correct, work 1 row.
**Now dec 1 st at neck edge on next row and every foll alt row until 21(24)sts remain.
Cont straight in patt until front measures the same as back to shoulder shaping, ending at side edge.

Shape shoulder
Keeping patt correct, cast off 7(8)sts at beg of next row and 2 foll alt rows.
With WS facing rejoin yarn to neck edge of rem sts and work as for first side from ** to end.

SLEEVES

Make 2. With 4½mm needles and A, cast on 40 sts and work cuff as follows:

Row 1: *K1A, K1B, rep from * to end.

Row 2: *P1B, P1A, rep from * to end.

Rep last 2 rows until cuff measures 7cm (3in) from cast-on edge, ending with a 2nd row.

Increase row: (RS facing) *In A (K1, P1, K1) into next st, K1B, rep from * to end of row – 80 sts.

Now starting with the 2nd row, work in patt as for back, inc 1 st at both ends of 3rd row and then every foll 4th row until there are 92 sts on the needle, working inc sts into the patt.

Cont straight in patt until 6 rows of bobbles have been worked, ending with a 12th patt row (bobbles in E have just been worked).

Shape top

Keeping patt correct, cast off 10 sts at beg of next 2 rows – 72 sts.

Now dec 1 st at each end of 3rd row and then foll 4th row.

Rep these 7 rows until 40 sts remain.

Work a few rows straight until 10 rows of bobbles have been worked, ending with a 12th patt row (bobbles in C have just been worked). Cast off.

DECORATION

(Diagram 1) decorate all pieces with rhinestones alternating colours and placing on every other B stripe.

Cords

Make 4. It is easier if each cord is made separately. You need 4 cords, one for each side of front panel and one for each shoulder.

These are made as follows:

Take two 137cm (54in) lengths of each coloured yarn (10 lengths altogether) and knot the ends together. Place this knotted end under a heavy object or tie to a door knob.

Stand at a distance pulling yarn taut; now twist until yarns form a spiral cord. Fold in half and yarn will automatically wind around itself forming the cord.

Embroider rows of chain stitch in D across centre front panel (beg and end at centre of bobbles at sides), working over the A stripes and under the B stripes.

TO MAKE UP

Sew in all ends.

Attach cords neatly and carefully to either side of centre front panel being careful not to pull too tight (**Diagram 2**).

Join shoulder seams matching patts.

Set sleeves into armhole edges gathering up sleeve tops with a gathering thread and matching patts carefully.

Place cords over seams where sleeves join armholes. Stitch down carefully (**Diagram 3**).

Bell frilling

Alike. With 3¼mm needles and D, and RS facing, pick up and K40 sts evenly along bottom edge of one cuff. P1 row.

Row 1: (RS facing) K1, *P3, K1, rep from * to last 3 sts, P3.

Row 2: *K3, P1, rep from * to last 4 sts, K3, P1.

Row 3: K1, *P3, yon, K1, yon, rep from * to last 3 sts, P3.

Row 4: *K3, P3, rep from * to last 4 sts, K3, P1.

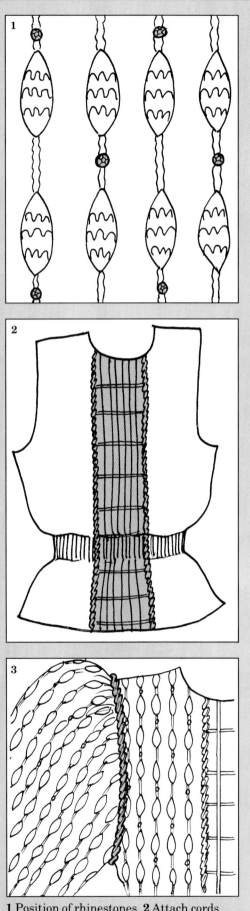

1 Position of rhinestones. **2** Attach cords and embroider chain stitch on front panel. **3** Place cord over shoulder seam.

Row 5: K1, *P3, yon, K3, yon, rep from * to last 3 sts, P3.
Row 6: *K3, P5, rep from * to last 4 sts, K3, P1.
Row 7: K1, *P3, yon, K5, yon, rep from * to last 3 sts, P3.
Row 8: *K3, P7, rep from * to last 4 sts, K3, P1.
Row 9: K1, *P3, yon, K7, yon, rep from * to last 3 sts, P3.
Row 10: *K3, P9, rep from * to last 4 sts, K3, P1.
Row 11: K1, *P3, yon, K9, yon, rep from * to last 3 sts, P3.
Row 12: *K3, P11, rep from * to last 4 sts, K3, P1.
Cast off all K sts in K and all P sts in P.

To complete

Join underarm and side seams, matching patterns carefully, and leave a side opening of 20cm (8in) in one side at point of waist shaping (**Diagram 4**). Sew 2 buttons onto waist opening and work 2 crochet button loops to correspond. Crochet a picot edging in D all around bottom edge.

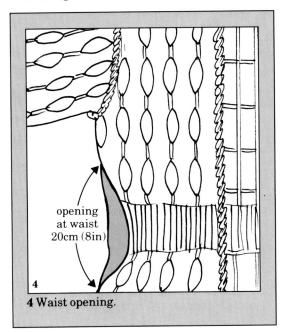

opening
at waist
20cm (8in)

4 Waist opening.

Neck ribbing

With the set of four 4½mm needles and A yarn used *double*, and RS facing, pick up and K 92 sts evenly around neck edge and work in rounds of K2, P2 rib as follows:
Work 4 rounds in A, 1 round in B, 4 rounds in A, 1 round in D, 4 rounds in A, 1 round in B, 4 rounds in A, 1 round in D.
Now work bell frilling, as on cuffs, for 10 rounds in D.
Cast off all K sts in K and all P sts in P.

VERSION 2

WITH GOLD BACKGROUND AND NO DECORATION

MATERIALS
Yarn
Use Aran weight: 300g(11oz) gold lurex worked double (A), 100g(4oz) black wool (B), 150g(6oz) each of red mohair (C), green wool (D), blue mohair (E)
Needles and tension as for Version 1.
Work as for Version 1, but use different arrangement of colours as given above.
Work bell frilling on neck and cuffs in blue (E) instead of gold.
Omit all rhinestone decoration and cording.

VERSION 3

IN TWO COLOURS

MATERIALS
Yarn
Use Aran weight: 300g(11oz) black wool (A), 400g(15oz) green mohair (B), 100g(4oz) gold lurex worked double (C)
Needles and tension as for Version 1.
Work as for Version 1. Yarn A remains the same throughout, but yarn B is used instead of yarns C, D and E, except for bell frilling which is worked in gold (C) as for Version 1.
When making cords use four 137 (54in) lengths of each of the three yarns (black, green and gold).
Omit all rhinestone decoration.

Version 2: the background changes to gold lurex for this sweater with the bobble stitch worked in red, green and blue.

Version 3: sweater worked in black and green only with gold lurex used for the neck and cuff frilling and in the cording.

RENAISSANCE SKULL CAP

MEASUREMENTS (see also page 168)
One size only: to fit average size adult head

VERSION 1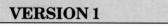

MATERIALS
Yarn
Use double-knit weight: 20g(1oz) black wool and 20g(1oz) gold lurex used together throughout (A), 10g(½oz) blue mohair (B), 10g(½oz) green wool (C)
Needles
1 pair of 4½mm (US 7) needles
For decoration
20 small red clip-on rhinestones
10 small blue clip-on rhinestones

Tension
18 sts and 24 rows to 10cm (4in) on 4½mm needles over st st.

> **NOTES**
>
> ● Any double-knit weight yarn can be used, as long as the tension is the same as that given.
>
> ● When working in more than one colour, strand yarn not in use loosely across wrong side of work over not more than 3 sts at a time to keep fabric elastic. The black and gold yarns are used *together* throughout, referred to as A.

METHOD
With 4½mm needles and A, cast on 80 sts and starting with a K row work 6 rows in st st.
Now work in bobble and stripe pattern as follows:
Row 1: (RS facing) *K3A, K1C, rep from * to end.
Row 2: *P1C, P3A, rep from * to end.
Rows 3 and 4: Rep 1st and 2nd rows once more.
Row 5: *K3A, in B (K1, P1, K1, P1) into next st, rep from * to end.
Row 6: *In B (K1, yon) 3 times and K1 over the 4 bobble sts, P3A, rep from * to end.
Row 7: *K3A, K4B (dropping yon sts), rep from * to end.
Row 8: *In B K2 tog twice, P3A, rep from * to end.
Row 9: *K3A, K2 tog B, rep from * to end.
Row 10: *P1C, P3A, rep from * to end.
Row 11: *K3A, K1C, rep from * to end.
Rows 12-16: Rep last 2 rows twice, then row 10 once.
Row 17: *K1A, K2 tog A, K1C, rep from * to end – 60 sts.
Row 18: *P1C, P2A, rep from * to end.
Row 19: *K2A, K1C, rep from * to end.
Row 20: As row 18.
Rows 21-24: Rep last 2 rows twice.
Row 25: *K2 tog A, K1C, rep from * to end – 40 sts.
Row 26: *P1C, P1A, rep from * to end.
Row 27: *K1A, K1C, rep from * to end.
Rows 28-32: Rep last 2 rows twice, then row 26 once.

Row 33: In C K2 tog all along row – 20 sts.
Now work 4 rows in st st in C.
Next row: K2 tog in C across row – 10 sts.
Thread yarn through rem sts and pull tight. Sew side seam together allowing cast-on edge to fall onto right side. Decorate with rhinestones or beads, dotting them at equal intervals along the vertical C stripes as required.

VERSION 2

STRIPED SKULL CAP

MATERIALS
Yarn
Use double-knit weight: 20g(1oz) black wool and 20g(1oz) gold lurex used together throughout (A), 20g(1oz) green wool (C)
Needles and tension as for Version 1

METHOD
With 4½mm needles and A, cast on 80 sts and work as for Version 1 to 4th patt row.
Now, instead of working bobbles, repeat rows 3 and 4 three times.
Follow on from row 11 to match Version 1.

VERSION 3

PLAIN SKULL CAP

MATERIALS
Yarn
Use double-knit weight: 30g(2oz) black wool and 30g(2oz) gold lurex used together throughout (A)
Needles and tension as for Version 1.

METHOD
With 4½mm needles and A, cast on 80 sts and starting with a K row work in st st for 11.5cm (4½in), ending with a WS row.
Next row: *K2, K2 tog. Rep from * to end of row – 60 sts.
Now work a further 2.5cm (1in) in st st in A, ending with a RS row.
Next row: *P1, P2 tog. Rep from * to end of row – 40 sts.
Next row: K2 tog along row – 20 sts.
Work 4 rows in st st.
Next row: P2 along row – 10 sts.
Thread yarn through rem sts and pull tight.
Join side seam.

Skull-cap hat knitted in a mixture of black wool and gold lurex. There are three styles: plain, striped and striped with a bobble-stitch band and decoration of tiny rhinestones.

RENAISSANCE SWEATER II

MEASUREMENTS (see also page 169)

Three sizes	small	medium	large
To fit bust:	81-86cm (32-34in)	91-97cm (36-38in)	97-102cm (38-40in)
Actual measurement:	94cm (37in)	100cm (39½in)	106cm (41¾in)
Length from shoulder:	61cm (24in)	64cm (25¼in)	67 cm (26½in)
Sleeve seam:	38cm (15in)	41cm (16¼in)	44cm (17½in)

VERSION 1

MATERIALS
Yarn
Use double-knit weight: 325(350 : 375)g/
12(13 : 14)oz 3-ply black lurex worked double (A),
325(350 : 375)g/12(13 : 14)oz gold silk (B)

Needles
1 pair each of 3¾mm (US 5) and 4mm (US 6)
needles
1 3¾mm (US 5) circular needle, *or* set of four
3¾mm (US 5) needles for neckband

For decoration
1½ metres each of two different patterned nets
(referred to as main net and contrast net)
70 clear small sew-on rhinestones
2 × metre lengths of pearls on gold chain, *or* 150
separate pearls
70 separate pearls
Reel of stretch cotton in matching colour
Shirring elastic for waist

Tension
28 sts and 26 rows to 10cm (4in) on 4mm needles
over Fair Isle pattern

opposite
Version 1: a sparkling
evening sweater knitted in
gold silk and black lurex,
decorated with net, pearls
and rhinestones, and with a
'ruff' collar made from net.

KEY

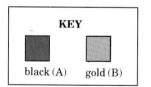

black (A)   gold (B)

NOTES

● Any double-knit weight yarn can be
used as long as the tension is the same as
that given.

● The black lurex should be worked *double*
throughout.

● It is easier to decorate the pieces flat
before sewing them together.

● When working from chart, strand yarn
not in use loosely across wrong side of work
over not more than 3 sts at a time to keep
fabric elastic.

BACK
With 3¾mm needles and A double, cast on
132(140 : 148) sts and starting with a K row work
7 rows in st st.
Fold-line row: (WS facing) K.
Change to 4mm needles and starting with a K
row, work in st st from chart as follows: On K
rows work 0(4 : 8) sts before the dotted line, rep
the sts between the dotted lines to last 17(21 :
2)sts, work 17(21 : 2) sts beyond the dotted line.
On P rows work 17(21 : 2)sts before the dotted
line, rep the sts between the dotted lines to last
0(4 : 8)sts, work 0(4 : 8) sts beyond the dotted line.
These 2 rows position the chart. Cont as set
repeating the 20 rows of chart until back
measures 33(36 : 39)cm/13(14¼ : 15½)in from
fold-line, ending with a WS row.

Shape armholes
Keeping patt correct, cast off 10(12 : 14)sts at beg
of next 2 rows – 112(116 : 120)sts.
Now dec 1 st at beg of next 16 rows – 96(100 :
104)sts.
Now cont straight in patt as set until back
measures 61(64 : 67)cm/24(25¼ : 26½)in from
fold-line, ending with a WS row.

Shape shoulders
Keeping patt correct, cast off 10 sts at beg of next
6 rows. Cast off rem 36(40 : 44)sts for back neck.

FRONT
Work exactly as for the back until front measures
51(54 : 57)cm/20 (21¼ : 22½)in from fold-line,
ending with a WS row.

Shape front neck
Next row: Patt 42 sts, cast off centre 12(16 :
20)sts, and patt to end and cont on this last set of
42 sts only.
**Keeping patt correct, dec 1 st at neck edge on
every row until 30 sts remain.
Now cont straight in patt until front measures
the same as back to shoulder shaping, ending at
side edge and on same patt row.

Shape shoulder
Keeping patt correct, cast off 10 sts at beg of next
row and foll 2 alt rows. With WS facing rejoin
yarn to rem sts at neck edge and work as for first
side from ** to end.

SLEEVES
Make 2. With 3¾mm needles and A yarn double,
cast on 76(80 : 84) sts and starting with a K row
work 7 rows in st st.
Fold-line row: (WS facing) K.
Change to 4mm needles and starting with a K
row work in st st from chart as follows: On K rows

CHART

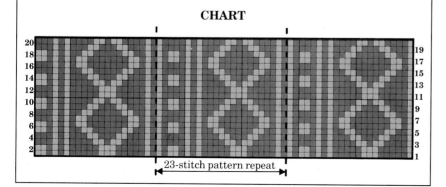

23-stitch pattern repeat

work 18(20 : 22)sts before the dotted line, rep the sts between the dotted lines to last 12(14 : 16)sts, work 12(14 : 16)sts beyond the dotted line. On P rows work 12(14 : 16)sts before the dotted line, rep the sts between the dotted lines to last 18(20 : 22)sts, work 18(20 : 22)sts beyond the dotted line. Work from chart as now set until row 16 has been worked.

Now keeping chart correct, inc 1 st at each end of next row and every foll 3rd row until there are 124(132 : 140)sts on the needle, working inc sts into the patt. Now cont straight in patt until sleeve measures 38 (41 : 44)cm/15 (16¼ : 17½)in from fold-line, ending with a WS row.

Shape top
Keeping patt correct, cast off 10(12 : 14)sts at beg of next 2 rows – 104(108 : 112)sts.
Now dec 1 st at each end of every row until 54(58 : 62)sts remain.
Cast off remaining sts.

TO MAKE UP
Sew in all ends and press pieces carefully on wrong side. Press hems on bottom edge and cuffs up onto wrong side and carefully slip stitch into position.

DECORATION
Front and back: Using the main net, cut into strips as follows: 4 strips 51cm (20in) long and 7.5cm (3in) wide; 4 strips 81cm (32in) long and 7.5cm (3in) wide.
Pin the strips of net loosely onto the vertical diamond patterns of back, so that fabric bubbles slightly between each pin (the net will be stretched when stitched onto knitting). Place the

4 × 81cm (32in) lengths on the longest part of the back and place the 2 × 51cm (20in) lengths on either side of the back and the front under armhole shaping **(Diagram 1)**.
Using stretch cotton stitch the net to the knitting with a row of machine stitching on either side, following the line of the pattern for accuracy, and stretching the knitting slightly as you stitch so that it will give the net a ruched effect.
Trim away the rough edges and cotton ends on the net **(Diagram 2)**.

Decorate front panel: Sew the rhinestones into the centres of the two diamond patterns on front **(Diagram 3)**. Stitch strings of pearls in between the diamond panels **(Diagram 4)**. If you cannot get lengths of pearls then stitch individual pearls in straight lines.

Net puffs: Cut 2 lengths of main net 81cm (32in) × 12.5cm (5in) wide. Cut 2 lengths of contrast net 81cm (32in) × 12.5cm (5in) wide.
Place 1 strip of main net and 1 strip of contrast net together with the contrast net on the top. Now pinch net into puffs at 6cm (2½in) intervals and stitch around with matching thread, pulling the net into a tight gathered puff. Finish each puff by stitching a pearl to the gathered section **(Diagram 5)**. Attach puffs to front, placing one on each side of centre panel of rhinestones and pearls **(Diagram 6)**, by stitching puffs lightly onto the front at position behind gathered area so that puff remains free.

To narrow the waist: Work two rows of shirring elastic in matching colour by hand across back of work along required waistline, approx 15cm (6in) up from fold-line, on both back and front. Gather

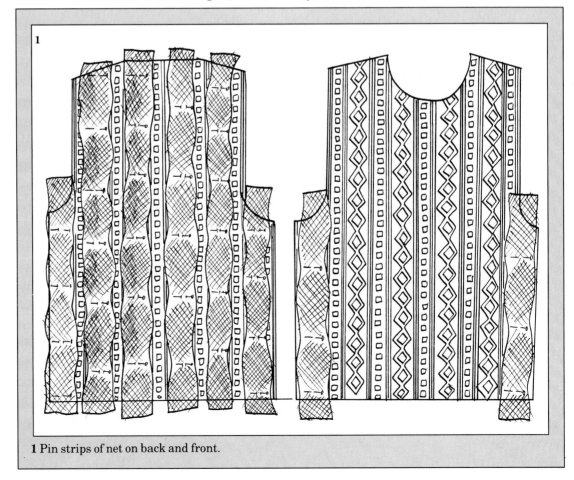

1 Pin strips of net on back and front.

2 Trim away rough edges. **3** Decorate front with rhinestones. **4** Sew on strings of pearls. **5** Make net puffs.

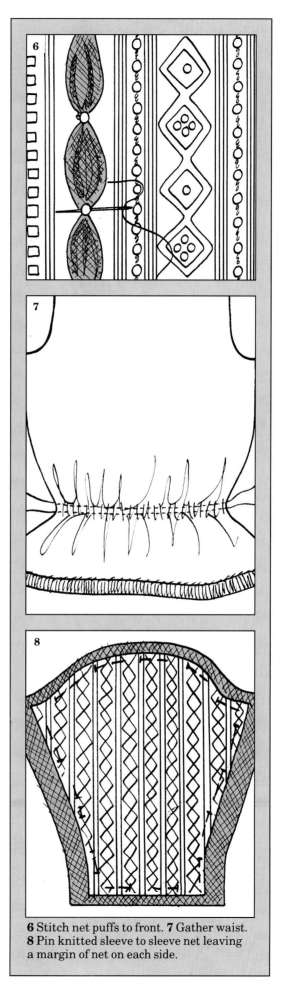

6 Stitch net puffs to front. **7** Gather waist. **8** Pin knitted sleeve to sleeve net leaving a margin of net on each side.

up to waist measurement required (**Diagram 7,** see page 75). Make sure that elastic does not show on right side of garment.

Sleeves: Lay the contrast net out flat and place sleeves on top, leaving 8cm (3in) of net on each side of sleeve and 2cm (¾in) at top and bottom. Pin sleeve to net and cut out net 8cm (3in) larger at sides and 2cm (¾in) longer at top and bottom (**Diagram 8,** see page 75).
Unpin net from sleeves.

Net puffs: Using the main net cut 6 lengths of 81cm (32in) × 10cm (4in) wide. Make net puffs as before using single net. Place three strips on top of sleeve net, one at centre sleeve and one either side (**Diagram 9**).
Stitch net puffs into place lightly, trim at each end to match sleeve net. Run a gathering thread through top of sleeve net and also at 9cm (3½in) up from bottom edge and gather both up until the net sleeve matches the knitted sleeve in size (leave a 1cm (½in) border of net all the way around).
Tack the net onto the knitting around the edges but leaving the cuff edge open (**Diagram 10**).

Gather cuffs: run two rows of shirring elastic through sleeve and net 8cm (3in) up from bottom edge, thus joining the 2 layers together and gather up to required cuff width.

To complete
Join shoulder seams enclosing overlapping net in between seams.
Join top sleeve edges to armhole (leave net puffs free over shoulders) easing top sleeve if necessary to fit armhole.
Join underarm and side seams matching patterns carefully.

Neckband
Using the 3¾mm circular needle, or the set of four 3¾mm needles and B, pick up and K36(40 : 44)sts across back neck, 14 sts at side front neck, 12(16 : 20)sts at centre front and 14 sts at other side of neck – 76(84 : 92)sts.
Work in rounds of K1, P1 rib in B for 2cm (¾in). Cast off loosely in rib.

Net collar
Using the contrast net cut as follows:
1 length of 142cm (56in) × 13cm (5in)
1 length of 142cm (56in) × 10cm (4in)
1 length of 142cm (56in) × 8cm (3in)
Pin all 3 strips together with narrowest strip on outside and machine stitch 2 rows of gathering sts along bottom edge.
Gather collar to approx 58cm (23in) – it has to be big enough to stretch with ribbed neckband over head (**Diagram 11**).
Carefully stitch net layers to inside of neckband, stretching band as you stitch (place opening in net at centre back neck).

Inner neck rib: With WS facing and using the 3¾mm circular needle, or the set of four 3¾mm needles and B, pick up and K 76(84 : 92)sts on inside of neck to match outer neck rib and work in K1, P1 rib to match.
Cast off loosely in rib.
Carefully stitch the two ribbed bands together sandwiching the gathered edge of the net collar in between (**Diagram 12** see page 78).

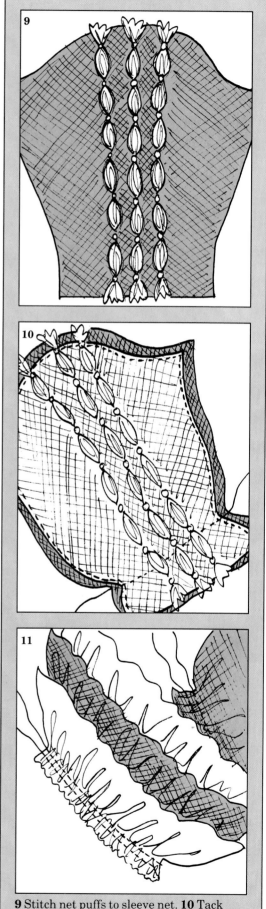

9 Stitch net puffs to sleeve net. **10** Tack sleeve net to knitted sleeve. **11** Gather net collar.

Version 2: sweater knitted in cream silk and gold lurex banded with rhinestones; the net 'ruff' collar completes the Renaissance look.

VERSION 2

WORKED IN CREAM SILK AND GOLD LUREX WITH NET RUFF COLLAR

MATERIALS
Yarn
Use double-knit weight: 325(350 : 375)g/
12(13 : 14)oz cream silk (A), 325(350 : 375)g/
12(13 : 14)oz 3-ply gold lurex worked double (B)
For decoration
500 small clear rhinestones
1½ metres of patterned net
Shirring elastic for waist
Needles and tension as for Version 1

METHOD
Work in pattern exactly as for Version 1, but in colours as above. Sew in ends and press. Omit all instructions for decoration and instead decorate all pieces with rhinestones **(Diagram 13)**. Run shirring elastic by hand around waistline and cuffs as for Version 1. Stitch garment together then follow instructions as for Version 1 for neckband, net collar and inner neck rib.

VERSION 3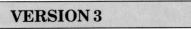

ALL WOOL UNDECORATED CREW-NECK SWEATER WITH RIBBED WELT

MATERIALS
Yarn
Use double-knit weight: 325(350 : 375)g/
12(13 : 14)oz black wool (A), 325(350 : 375)g/
12(13 : 14)oz magenta wool (B)
Needles
1 pair each of 3¼mm (US 3) and 4mm
(US 6) needles
Tension as for Version 1.

BACK
With 3¼mm needles and A, cast on 98 (104 : 110) sts and work in K1, P1 rib for 8cm (3in).
Increase row: Rib and inc 34 (36 : 38) sts evenly across row – 132(140 : 148)sts.
Change to 4mm needles and work from chart following all instructions as Version 1.

FRONT
Follow rib instructions as for back, then follow Version 1 instructions for front.

SLEEVES
Make 2. With 3¼mm needles and A, cast on 48 (52 : 56) sts and work in K1, P1 rib for 8cm (3in).
Increase row: Rib and inc 28 sts evenly across row – 76 (80 : 84) sts. Change to 4mm needles and work from chart and follow rest of sleeve instructions as for Version 1.

TO MAKE UP
Sew in ends and press pieces. Join shoulder seams. Join top sleeves to armhole edges. Join underarm and side seams, matching patterns carefully. Work neckband as for Version 1.

12 Sandwich net collar between the two ribbed neckbands. **13** Rhinestones on Version 2.

Version 3: the basic geometric pattern looks striking knitted in black and magenta in this wool crew-neck style.

CAVALIER
INTRODUCTION

In seventeenth-century England, dress had special significance: it was a statement of political loyalties. The Civil War, of 1642-1649, split the country in two: the Cavaliers fought for the monarchy and the established order, with the style of life and dress that went with it; their opponents, the 'Roundheads' or Parliamentary forces, fought to establish a more democratic and puritanical state, and expressed their moral and political convictions by the simplicity and plainness of their clothes.

In the superficial version of history retained by most British school-children, the Cavalier appears as a light-hearted, dashing gallant. A typical figure is the romantic but ineffectual Rupert of the Rhine, nephew of King Charles I and a Royalist general. He is said to have thrown himself so whole-heartedly into a cavalry charge at the Battle of Edgehill that he chased his enemy out of sight and lost his military advantage – displaying more style than strategy. The Roundhead on the other hand is portrayed as virtuous but dull, a humourless killjoy. Unfair and simplistic though such

Elaborate Italian collar lace of about 1630-40 with the typical 'Vandyke' edging.

judgements may be, they are too well entrenched in the popular imagination to be easily dispelled. Certainly the Cavalier style of dress as shown by artists like Van Dyck and Mytens supports the romantic image.

Style in the seventeenth century – as so often in the history of European fashion – was set by the French. Their influence can be seen in the looser, more comfortable clothes which contrasted with the rigidly formal Spanish style of preceding years. (The Puritans rejected this French frivolity and favoured the more sober Dutch style of dress.) But the French fashions were not excessively flamboyant: Richelieu, chief minister of Louis XIII, the second half of whose reign was contemporary with that of Charles I in England, banned the import of gold and silver cloth and opulent trimmings. His purpose was to curb expenditure on dress, particularly if only foreigners were profiting from it. These strictures initially encouraged a rich simplicity of dress, though they resulted eventually in increased native production of lace, braid and other luxury materials. Along with the greater informality, men's dress had a certain military air, gained from the combination of breeches with wide-topped boots and a broad-brimmed hat – a swashbuckling look typified by the romantic heroes of Alexandre Dumas's *The Three Musketeers*.

The basic garment for men throughout the seventeenth century was the doublet and it is on this that the Cavalier Jacket (see photograph, page 83) is based. The doublet

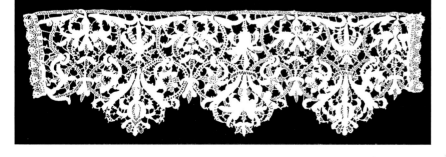

was at first worn with hose, but these were gradually superseded by loose baggy breeches reaching below the knee and caught in with ribbons or lace garters. A short cloak was often worn over the doublet, and at some periods an over-waistcoat or jerkin. Another waistcoat, or under-doublet, was often worn underneath the unfastened doublet so that the waistcoat was exposed to view. The sleeves of the doublet were wide and padded with stuffing, and in the early part of the century 'wings' or broad shoulder bands, often padded and embroidered, were worn to emphasize the shoulder line.

As in earlier periods, the doublet was often slashed at back and front and on the sleeves to reveal a contrasting lining or a shirt of fine white lace or cambric. This style was not purely decorative, but had a social significance: to keep white linen clean was expensive and laborious, so its display was the mark of a gentleman, proving that the wearer did not engage in dirty manual tasks. The sleeve narrowed at the wrist and was finished with a turned-back cuff, often trimmed with lace.

The large, elaborately wired ruffs of the Elizabethan age were replaced first by simpler, smaller, starched ones, which were in turn succeeded by 'falling ruffs', several layers of linen or lawn often edged with lace and set on to a high neckband, tied in front with 'bandstrings'. But even this simpler type of ruff was eventually replaced by a broad plain collar edged with or made entirely of lace and known as the 'falling band', reaching from neck almost to shoulder.

The Cavalier Jacket faithfully imitates the seventeenth-century doublet. Knitted in dark brown chenille with broad decorative shoulder bands and contrasting lace slashes, it comes close to the swaggering, masculine style of the times. Its chenille yarn gives the lustrous effect of velvet, a favourite fabric of the day. Lace trimming on the broad white collar and turned back cuffs completes the Cavalier look.

There was a passion for lace in the first half of the seventeenth century, and its use was probably more lavish on men's clothes than on women's. Both sexes wore the large collars and lace cuffs; but lace also embellished men's cloaks, breeches and gloves and even cascaded over the turned-down tops of their boots. It was much prized – Venetian lace was probably the finest – and could be almost as valuable as jewellery.

The lacy theme is taken up for the Lace Cardigan (see photograph, page 91), which is knitted in pale blue silk in an all-over

open-work pattern. Silk was a favourite material for fashionable clothes and light blues were popular shades; the cardigan's full sleeves are reminiscent of those of the Cavalier ladies' dresses.

On the cardigan, collar and cuff edgings are knitted in white cotton with a deeply cut edge imitating a style of collar lace which was very popular between 1625 and 1635. Sitters to the most famous portraitist of the day often wore such collars, hence the name, 'Vandyke' collar.

Accompanying the cardigan is the Brocade Waistcoat (see photograph, page 91), knitted in dusky pink mohair and black Aran wool. The patterning recalls the rich colour and texture of fine Italian silk brocade, another authentic material of Cavalier dress, which must rank as one of the most dashing and attractive styles in costume history.

Lord John and Lord Bernard Stuart (1638) by Van Dyck. The Stuart brothers wear the sumptuous silks and laces of the Cavaliers. They were Royalist officers and both were killed in the Civil War.

CAVALIER JACKET

MEASUREMENTS (see also page 169)

One size	medium
To fit bust:	81-91cm (32-36in)
Actual measurement (omitting lace insets):	110cm (43½in)
Length from shoulder: (including bottom ribbing):	66cm (26in)
Sleeve seam:	46cm (18in)

VERSION 1

MATERIALS
Yarn
628g (23oz) brown chenille – chunky Aran weight (A), 75g (3oz) black Aran (B), 90g (4oz) white cotton DK (C), 10g (½oz) gold lurex worked double (D)

> **NOTE**
> ● Any chunky Aran-weight yarn can be used, as long as the tension is the same as that given below.

Needles and other materials
1 pair each of 4½mm (US 7) and 5mm (US 8) needles
8 buttons
Shirring elastic (optional)
2 spare needles
2 safety pins
For decoration
5 metres of 10cm (4in) wide cotton lace
3 metres of 4cm (1½in) wide cotton lace

Tension
15 sts and 20 rows to 10cm (4in) on 5mm needles and st st using A.

RIGHT FRONT
Wth 5mm needles and A, cast on 40 sts and starting with a K row work straight in st st until front measures 15cm (6in) from cast-on edge, ending with a WS row.

Shape waist
Next row: K2 tog across row – 20 sts.
Starting with a P row work 3 rows in st st.
Next row: (RS facing) K twice into every st across row – 40 sts.
Starting with a P row cont straight in st st until front measures 28cm (11in) from cast-on edge, ending with a WS row.

Divide for first slash opening
Next row: K10 sts, leave these sts on a spare needle and cont on rem 30 sts only as follows:
Cont straight in st st until strip measures 36cm (14in) from cast-on edge, ending with a RS row (armhole edge).

Shape armhole
Cast off 6 sts at beg of next row – 24 sts.
Now dec 1 st at armhole edge on foll alt rows until 20 sts remain, ending with a WS row.

opposite
Version 1: Cavalier-style jacket knitted in chunky brown chenille with white lace slashes and lace-trimmed collar and cuffs. The gold of the filigree buttons is repeated in the shoulder rouleaus.

Divide for second slash opening
Next row: K 10 sts, leave these sts on another spare needle and cont on rem 10 sts only and work straight in st st until strip measures 48cm (19in) from cast-on edge, ending with a WS row, break yarn and leave sts on a safety pin.
With WS facing return to the middle set of 10 sts left on spare needle and work straight in st st on these sts until strip measures 48cm (19in) from cast-on edge, ending with a WS row, break yarn and leave sts on a safety-pin.
With WS facing return to rem set of 10 sts and work straight in st st on these sts until strip measures 48cm (19in) from cast-on edge, ending with a WS row. (All three pieces are the same length – see **Diagram 1**.)
With RS facing, K across all three strips of 10 sts – 30 sts.
Cont straight on these sts in st st until front measures 54cm (21in) from cast-on edge, ending at front edge.

Shape front neck
Cast off 6 sts at beg of next row – 24 sts.
Now dec 1 st at neck edge on every row until 18 sts remain.
Work a few rows straight in st st until front measures 63cm (25in) from cast-on edge, ending at armhole edge.

Shape shoulder
Cast off 6 sts at beg of next row and foll 2 alt rows.

LEFT FRONT
Work as for right front but reverse position of slashes by beginning to divide when the wrong side is facing and reverse armhole, neck and shoulder shapings.

BACK
With 5mm needles and A cast on 84 sts and starting with a K row work straight in st st until back measures 15cm (6 in) from cast-on edge, ending with a WS row.

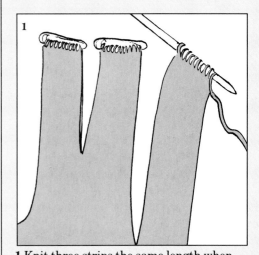

1 Knit three strips the same length when working fronts.

Shape waist
Next row: K2 tog across row – 42 sts.
Starting with a P row work 3 rows in st st.
Next row: (RS facing) K twice into every st across row – 84 sts.
Starting with a P row cont straight in st st until back measures 28cm (11in) from cast-on edge, ending with a WS row.

Divide for slash openings
(NB use four separate balls of A)
Next row: (RS facing) K26, drop yarn, then with a new ball K16, then with a new ball K16, then with a new ball K26.
Work straight in st st on these four separate strips, but work them all on the same needle, knitting each one with its own ball of yarn (or if you prefer, they can each be knitted separately as on the fronts.)
Work straight on these four strips until back measures 36cm (14in) from cast-on edge ending with a WS row.

Shape armholes
(worked on the two outside strips)
Next row: Cast off 6 sts, K20, K16, K16, K26.
Next row: Cast off 6 sts, P20, P16, P16, P20.
Now dec 1 st at beg of every row (working on 2 outside strips only) until you have 16 sts on each end strip (all 4 strips now have 16 sts) – 64 sts **(Diagram 2)**.
Now cont straight working strips separately as before, until all strips measure 48cm (19in) from cast-on edge, ending with a WS row.
Now K across all four strips. Work straight in st st on these 64 sts until back measures the same as front to shoulder shaping, ending with a WS row.

Shape shoulders
Cast off 6 sts at beg of next 6 rows.
Cast off rem 28 sts for back neck.

SLEEVES
Make 2. With 5mm needles and A, cast on 48 sts and starting with a K row work straight in st st until sleeve measures 5cm (2in) from cast-on edge, ending with a WS row.

Divide for slash openings
(NB use four separate balls of A)
Next row: (RS facing) K12, K12, K12, K12.
Cont to work each strip separately and inc 1 st at each end of each 12-st strip on 3rd and foll 4th rows until each strip has 20 sts (80 sts in all).
Cont straight in st st on these four separate 20-st strips until sleeve measures 41cm (16in) from cast-on edge, ending with a WS row.
Now K across all four strips – 80 sts.
Work straight in st st until sleeve measures 46cm (18in) from cast-on edge, ending with a WS row.
Cast off.

TO MAKE UP
Sew in all ends and gently press pieces on wrong side paying special attention to the edges of the slash openings.

Lace insets
(NB velvet, silk or suede could also be used)
Sleeves
Cut six lengths of lace 41cm (16in) long (i.e. 5cm/2in longer than slash openings). Gather up each end of the lace **(Diagram 3)**.

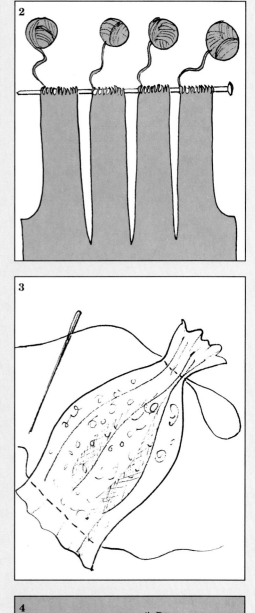

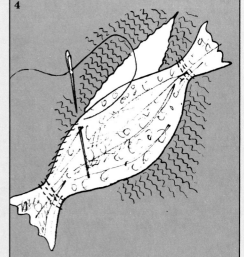

2 Knit four strips the same length when working back. **3** Gather up each end of lace insets. **4** Carefully stitch the edges of the lace insets to the edges of the openings.

Pin lace inserts on wrong side of sleeves placing edges of lace to edges of slash opening so that the lace will puff through the opening and show on the right side. Carefully stitch the edges of the lace to the edges of the opening **(Diagram 4)**. (NB use a matching colour in a finer yarn and be careful that the stitches do not show through onto the right side of the garment.)
Stitch through the top and bottom of slash on right side of sleeve to make the lace stand out more **(Diagram 5)**.

Back and fronts
Repeat the same process as for the sleeves cutting lengths of lace 5cm (2in) longer than the openings.

Cuffs
Alike. With 4½mm needles and B and RS facing, pick up and K40 sts evenly along bottom edge of one sleeve and work in K1, P1 rib for 6 rows.
Next row: (WS facing) K in C.
Next row: K in C for fold-line of cuff.
Now starting with a K row, work 12 rows in st st in C.
Work 2 rows in A. Work 4 rows in C.
Cast off in C.
Press the cuff.

Lace edgings
Alike. For each cuff you need one 46cm (18in) length of 4cm (1½in) lace. Gather up lace to fit edge of cuff. Pin and stitch lace onto bottom of cuff on inside **(Diagram 6)**.

Decorative front side ribs
Alike. (These are picked up and knitted vertically on fronts.)
Right side: With RS facing count 10 sts in from the side edge just under the armhole shaping. Now from edge of armhole, 10 sts in from side edge, and with 4½mm needles and B, pick up and K 64 sts from this point following the stitches down to the bottom edge.
Work 6 rows in K1, P1 rib in B.
Cast off loosely in rib.

Left side: Work as for right side, but pick up stitches from bottom edge to armhole edge.
Join shoulder seams together.
Join top sleeve edges to armhole edges.
Join underarm and side seams.
Join cuff edges neatly on wrong side and then fold cuffs back onto right side of sleeves.
Slip stitch top edge of cuff lightly to bottom sleeve **(Diagram 7)**.

Button band
With 4½mm needles and RS facing and B, pick up and K86 sts evenly along centre front edge of left front and work in K1, P1 rib for 8 rows.
Cast off loosely in rib.

Buttonhole band
Pick up sts as for button band, but along right front edge.
Work 3 rows in K1, P1 rib.
Next row: (RS facing) Rib 9, *cast off 3 sts, rib 7, rep from * to last 7 sts, cast off 3 sts, rib 4.
Next row: Rib, casting on 3 sts over cast-off sts on previous row (8 buttonholes worked).
Work 3 more rows in rib.
Cast off loosely in rib. Press ribs and front edges.

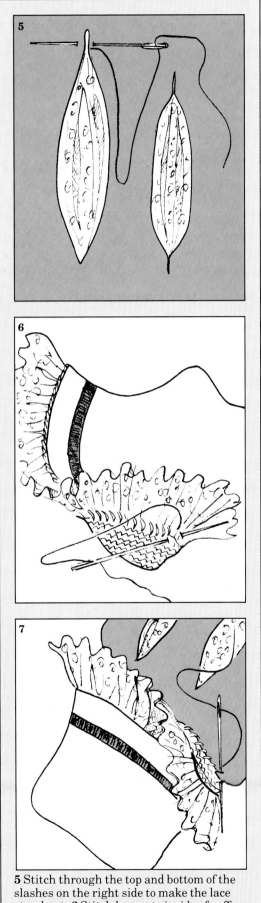

5 Stitch through the top and bottom of the slashes on the right side to make the lace stand out. **6** Stitch lace onto inside of cuff. **7** Slip stitch top edge of cuff lightly to bottom sleeve.

85

Bottom ribbing

(NB pick up through both the decorative side ribs (which face towards side edge) and the button/buttonhole bands to hold in place **Diagram 8**).
With 4½mm needles and B and with RS facing, pick up and K42 sts from centre front to side seam, 72 sts across back and 42 sts across other front – 156 sts.
Work 6 rows in K1, P1 rib in B.
Cast off loosely in rib.
Press rib and bottom edge.

Shoulder rouleaus

Make 2. With 4½mm needles and B, cast on 14 sts and work in stripe and bobble pattern as follows:
Row 1: (RS facing) K in B.
Row 2: P in B.
Row 3: K1B, *now in D make bobble as follows: (K1, P1, K1, P1, K1) into next st, then slip the 2nd, 3rd, 4th and 5th sts over the top of the 1st st, K3B, rep from * to last st, K1B.
Row 4: P in B.
Row 5: K in C.
Row 6: P in C.
Row 7: *K3C, make bobble in B, rep from * to last 2 sts, K2C.
Row 8: P in C.
These 8 rows form the pattern and are repeated as required.
Cont straight in patt as set until work fits around armhole edge (approx 58cm/23in long).
Cast off.
Sew in all ends and join long seams rouleaus; carefully stitch them from the outside (the seams will not show as they will be concealed when rouleaus are sewn around armholes).
Now stitch rouleaus on top of armhole seam all the way round (**Diagram 9**) and join ends together at underarm.

Collar

With 4½mm needles and B, and with RS facing and starting half-way across buttonhole band, pick up and K 24 sts to shoulder seam, 26 sts across back neck and 24 sts across other front to centre of button band – 74 sts.
Work 4 rows in K1, P1 rib in B.
Next row: (WS facing) K in C.
Next row: K in C for fold-line of collar.
Starting with a K row work 10 rows in st st in C.
Increase row: K1, *K1, (K1, P1) into next st, rep from * to last st, K1 – 110 sts.
Starting with a P row cont in st st in C for another 11 rows.
Work 2 rows in st st in A. Work 4 rows in st st in C.
Cast off in C. Sew in ends, press collar.

Lace edging

You will need 2m of 4cm (1½in) lace (same as cuffs).
Gather up lace with gathering thread until it fits along the edge of the collar and around the sides at front. Spread out gathers evenly and pin lace to edge of collar on underside; stitch on carefully.
The collar can be left flat or it can be folded along the increase line to make it stand up and then lightly stitched on either side of neck to hold it in place (**Diagram 10**).
To give the jacket more shape, a length of shirring elastic may be threaded through the decrease row at waist level and secured at each end.
Sew on buttons to correspond to buttonholes.

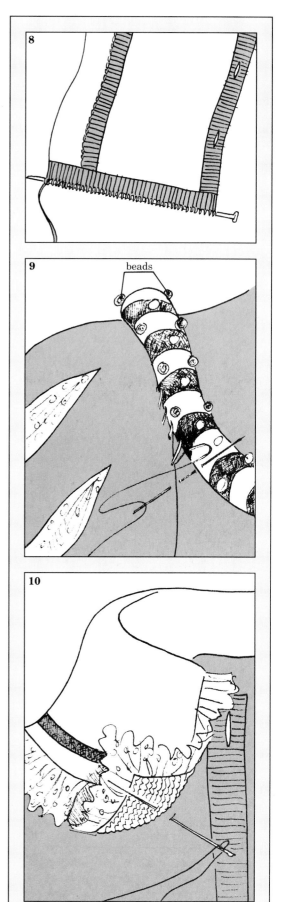

8 Bottom ribbing 9 Stitch rouleau all the way round armhole seam. 10 Stitch collar lightly on either side of the neck to hold it in place.

Version 2: the jacket is knitted in black Aran wool with lace-trimmed collar and cuffs and decorative rouleaus, but without the slashes.

VERSION 2

PLAIN BLACK JACKET WITH DECORATIVE COLLAR, CUFFS AND ROULEAUS

MATERIALS
Yarn
700g (25oz) black Aran (A), 90g (4oz) white cotton DK (C), 10g (½oz) gold lurex used double (D)
Needles and tension as for Version 1.
For decoration
3 metres of 4cm (1½in) wide cotton lace

RIGHT FRONT
With 4½mm needles and A, cast on 40 sts and work in K1, P1 rib for 2.5cm (1in).
Change to 5mm needles and starting with a K row work straight in st st until front measures 15cm (6in) from top of ribbing, ending with a WS row. Work waist shaping as for **Version 1**. Then cont straight in st st in A until front measures 36cm (14in) from top of ribbing, ending with a RS row (armhole edge).

Shape armhole
Cast off 6 sts at beg of next row – 34 sts.
Now dec 1 st at armhole edge on foll alt rows until 30 sts remain. Now cont straight in st st until front measures 54cm (21in) from top of ribbing, ending at front edge.

Shape front neck
Cast off 6 sts at beg of next row – 24 sts.
Now dec 1 st at neck edge on every row until 18 sts remain. Work a few rows straight until front measures 63cm (25in) from top of ribbing, ending at armhole edge.

Shape shoulder
Cast off 6 sts at beg of next row and foll 2 alt rows.

LEFT FRONT
Work as for right front but reverse all shapings.

BACK
With 4½mm needles and A, cast on 84 sts and work in K1, P1 rib for 2.5cm (1in).
Change to 5mm needles and starting with a K row work straight in st st until back measures 15cm (6in) from top of ribbing ending with a WS row. Work waist shaping as for Version 1.
Now cont straight in st st until back measures 36cm (14in) from top of ribbing ending with a WS row.

Shape armholes
Cast off 6 sts at beg of next 2 rows.
Dec 1 st at beg of next 8 rows – 64 sts.
Now cont straight until back measures the same as front to shoulder shaping ending with a WS row.

Shape shoulders
Cast off 6 sts at beg of next 6 rows.
Cast off rem 28 sts for back neck.

SLEEVES
Make 2. With 5mm needles and A, cast on 48 sts and starting with a K row cont straight in st st until sleeve measures 5 cm (2in) from cast-on edge, ending with a WS row.
Increase row: Inc 1 st st in every 2nd st of row – 72 sts.
Cont in st st in A and inc 1 st at each end of 3rd

and foll 4th rows until 80 sts are on the needle. Now cont straight in st st until sleeve measures 46cm (18in) from cast-on edge, ending with a WS row. Cast off.

Sew in ends and press pieces.
Work decorative cuffs and lace edgings as Version 1.
Omit side ribs and bottom ribs. Join seams.
Work front bands as Version 1, but pick up and K 90 sts evenly along centre front edge (this includes bottom ribbing). Work shoulder rouleaus as Version 1.
Work collar and complete as Version 1.

VERSION 3

BLUE CHENILLE JACKET WITH LACE INSETS, RIBBED NECK AND CUFFS

MATERIALS
Yarn
750g (27oz) blue chenille (A)
Needles and tension as Version 1, but 9 buttons are needed.
For decoration
5 metres of 10cm (4in) wide cotton lace

RIGHT FRONT
With 4½mm needles and A, cast on 40 sts and work in K1, P1 rib for 2.5cm (1in).
Change to 5mm needles and starting with a K row work straight in st st until front measures 15cm (6in) from top of ribbing, ending with a WS row. Work waist shaping as for Version 1.
Now follow rest of instructions as for Version 1.

LEFT FRONT
Work as for right front but in reverse (as Version 1).

BACK
With 4½mm needles and A, cast on 84 sts and work in K1, P1 rib for 2.5cm (1in).
Change to 5mm needles and work as for Version 1, always measuring from top of ribbing.

SLEEVES
Make 2. With 4½mm needles and A, cast on 48 sts and work in K1, P1 rib for 2.5cm (1in).
Change to 5mm needles and follow instructions for Version 1.

Work making up instructions and lace insets as for Version 1. Omit cuffs and side ribs.
Join seams and insert sleeves.
Work front bands as Version 1.
Omit bottom ribbing, rouleaus and collar, but pick up and K90 sts evenly along centre front edge (this includes bottom ribbing).

NECK RIBBING
With 4½mm needles and A, and with RS facing and starting at very edge of buttonhole band, pick up and K 26 sts to shoulder seam, 26 sts across back neck and 26 sts to edge of button band – 78 sts. Work in K1, P1 rib in A for 3 rows.
Next row: (RS facing – buttonhole row) Rib 2, cast off 3 sts, rib to end.
Next row: Rib, casting on 3 sts over cast-off sts on previous row. Work 2 more rows in rib.
Cast off in rib.
Sew on buttons to correspond to buttonholes, and insert shirring elastic if required.

Version 3: blue chenille cardigan with lace slashes.

LACE CARDIGAN

MEASUREMENTS (see also page 169)

Three sizes	small	medium	large
To fit bust:	81-86cm (32-34in)	91-97cm (36-38in)	102-107cm (40-42in)
Actual measurement:	100cm (39½in)	108cm (42½in)	116cm (45½in)
Length from shoulder:	58cm (23in)	61cm (24in)	63cm (25in)
Sleeve seam			
(omitting cuff):	33cm (13in)	35cm (14in)	38cm (15in)

VERSION 1

MATERIALS

Yarn

Use double-knit weight.
625(650 : 675)g/22(23 : 24)oz blue silk (A), 125g
(4½oz) white cotton (B), small amount of
black (C)

Needles and other materials

1 pair each of 3¼mm (US 3) and 4mm (US 6)
needles
1 4mm (US 6) circular needle
8 buttons
Shirring elastic
2 safety pins

Tension

21 sts and 28 rows to 10cm (4in) on 4mm (US 6)
needles and main lace pattern.

NOTES

- Any double-knit weight yarn can be used
whether it be wool, silk or cotton as long as
the tension is the same as that given above.

- When working from chart, weave yarn in
at back of work over not more than 3 sts at
a time to keep fabric elastic.

BACK

With 3¼mm needles and A, cast on 109(115 :
121)sts and work in single rib as follows:
Row 1: (RS facing) K1, *P1, K1, rep from * to end.
Row 2: P1, *K1, P1, rep from * to end.
Rep last 2 rows until rib measures 2.5cm (1in),
ending with a 2nd row. Change to 4mm needles
and work in lace pattern as follows:
Row 1: (WS facing and all other WS rows) P.
Rows 2, 4 and 6: K1, *yf, s! 1, K1, psso, K1, K2
tog, yf, K1, rep from * to end.
Row 8: K2, *yf, sl 1, K2 tog, psso, yf, K3, rep from
* ending last rep with K2.
Row 10: K1, *K2 tog, yf, K1, yf, sl 1, K1, psso, K1,
rep from * to end.
Row 12: K2 tog, *yf, K3, yf, sl 1, K2 tog, psso,
rep from * ending last rep with yf, K3, yf, sl 1,
K1, psso. These 12 rows form the pattern and are
repeated throughout. Cont straight in patt as set
until back measures 30(33 : 35)cm/12(13 : 14)in
from cast-on edge, ending with a WS row.

Shape armholes

Cast off 10 sts at beg of next 2 rows – 89(95 :
101)sts.
Keeping patt correct, dec 1 st at each end of next

row and 5 foll alt rows – 77(83 : 89)sts.
Now cont straight in patt until back measures
58(61 : 63)cm/23(24 : 25)in from cast-on edge,
ending with a WS row.

Shape shoulders

Keeping patt correct, cast off 7(8 : 9)sts at beg of
next 6 rows.
Cast off rem 35 sts.

RIGHT FRONT

With 3¼mm needles and A, cast on 49(55 : 61)sts
and work in single rib as for back welt for 2.5cm
(1in) ending with a 2nd row.
Change to 4mm needles and work straight in patt
as given for back until front measures the same
as back to armhole shaping, ending with a RS
row, and on same patt row.

Shape armhole

Cast off 10 sts at beg of next row – 39(45 : 51)sts.
Now keeping patt correct, dec 1 st at armhole
edge on next row and then at this edge on 5 foll
alt rows – 33(39 : 45)sts.
Now cont straight in patt until front measures
51(54 : 56)cm/20(21 : 22)in from cast-on edge,
ending with a WS row.

Shape front neck

Cast off 8 sts at beg of next row – 25(31 : 37)sts.
Keeping patt correct, dec 1 st at neck edge on
every row until 21(24 : 27)sts remain.
Now cont straight in patt until front measures
the same as back to shoulder shaping, ending on
same patt row, and at armhole edge.

Shape shoulder

Cast off 7(8 : 9)sts at beg of next row and foll 2
alt rows.

LEFT FRONT

Work as for right front but reversing all shapings.

SLEEVES

Make 2. With 4mm needles and A, cast on 85 sts
and work in pattern as for back, but working
extra sts into the patt at the same time by
increasing 1 st at each end of every foll alt row
until 151 sts are on the needle.
Now cont straight in patt until sleeve measures
33(35 : 38)cm/13(14 : 15)in from cast-on edge,
ending with a WS row.

Shape top

Cast off 10 sts at beg of next 2 rows – 131 sts.
Now keeping patt correct, dec 1 st at each end of
every row until 47 sts remain.
Cast off.

opposite
*Version 1: pretty lacy blue
cardigan with Cavalier-
style collar and cuffs is
worn with a warm brocade
pattern waistcoat in pink
mohair and black wool
with a black and white
picot border.*

LACE CUFFS

Make 2. With 4mm needles and B, cast on 10 sts.
Row 1: Sl 1, K2, yf, K2 tog, K1, (yf and over needle twice, K2 tog) twice.
Row 2: Sl 1, K1, P1, K2, P1, K3, yf, K2 tog, K1.
Row 3: Sl 1, K2, yf, K2 tog, K3, (yf and over needle twice, K2 tog) twice.
Row 4: Sl 1, K1, P1, K2, P1, K5, yf, K2 tog, K1.
Row 5: Sl 1, K2, yf, K2 tog, K5, (yf and over needle twice, K2 tog) twice.
Row 6: Sl 1, K1, P1, K2, P1, K7, yf, K2 tog, K1.
Row 7: Sl 1, K2, yf, K2 tog, K11.
Row 8: Cast off 6 sts, K6 (7 sts on RH needle), yf, K2 tog, K1.
These 8 rows form the pattern for the cuff and are repeated as required.
Cont straight in patt as set until cuff measures approx 25cm (10in) from cast-on edge, ending with an 8th patt row.
Cast off.

BUTTONHOLE BAND

With 3¼mm needles and A, cast on 9 sts and work in single rib as for back welt for 1cm (½in), ending with a WS row.
Next row: (buttonhole row) Rib 3, cast off 3 sts, rib 3.
Next row: Rib, casting on 3 sts over cast-off sts on previous row. Cont in rib. At the same time, work a further 6 buttonholes at 7.5 (8 : 8.5)cm/ 3(3¼ : 3½)in intervals (7 buttonholes worked in all).
Now work straight in rib until band reaches up right front to start of neck shaping when slightly stretched, ending with a WS row.
Leave sts on a safety-pin.

BUTTONBAND

Work as for buttonhole band but omitting all buttonholes.

TO MAKE UP

Press pieces gently on wrong side. As this garment is made of pure silk which has a tendency to stretch in wearing, it is advisable to stay-stitch around the edges of the pieces with a line of machine stitching in a matching colour as close to the edge as possible. Stay-stitch the underarm edges, side seams, armhole edges and centre front edges. This should prevent the garment 'growing' too much.
Attach lace cuffs to bottom sleeve edges:
Run a gathering thread through the bottom edge of the sleeve and gather it up until it measures the same length as the lace cuff, i.e. approx 25cm (10in). Stitch cuff onto bottom edge of sleeve. Join shoulder seams together. Gather top of sleeve with gathering thread until it fits into armhole, then pin carefully and place the majority of the gathers over the top shoulder area so they puff up. Stitch in position. Join underarm and side seams and cuff edges. Attach bands to centre front edges. Press. Run a length of shirring elastic through the cuffs at the point where the lace cuff joins the sleeve, to give added shape.

Neckband

With 3¼mm needles and A and with RS facing, rib across the 9 sts of buttonhole band, then pick up and K 20 sts around front neck, 25 sts at back neck and 20 sts from around second front neck and rib across the 9 sts of other front band – 83 sts.

Starting with the 2nd row work in single rib as for back welt for 3 rows.
Next row: (RS facing, buttonhole row) Rib 3, cast off 3 sts, rib to end.
Next row: Rib, casting on 3 sts over cast-off sts on previous row. Work 2 more rows in rib.
Cast off neatly in rib.

Collar

Using the 4mm circular needle and B, cast on 150 sts and work in pattern and rows as follows:
Starting with a K row work 2 rows in st st in B.
Now work from chart as follows: On K rows rep the 7-stitch patt between the dotted lines to last 3 sts, work 3 sts beyond the dotted line. On P rows work 3 sts before the dotted line, work the 7-stitch patt repeat to end.
Cont as set until the 12 rows of the chart have been worked.
Row 13: (RS facing) Decrease row: In B, *K1, K2 tog, rep from * to end – 100 sts.
Row 14: P in B.
Row 15: K2B, *K2A, K3B, rep from * ending last rep with K1B.
Row 16: P in B.
Row 17: K in B.
Row 18: P in B.
Row 19: *K2A, K3B, rep from * to end.
Row 20: P in B.
Row 21: (Decrease row) in B, *K3, K2 tog, rep from * to end – 80 sts.
Row 22: P in B.
Cast off in B.
Sew in ends and press collar.

Decorative collar edging

Work the same lace edging as for cuffs and cont straight until edging measures the same as the outer edge of collar, approx 81cm (32in), ending with an 8th patt row. Cast off.
Carefully stitch lace edging onto outer edge of collar (**Diagram 1**). Press edge of collar.

To complete

Slightly gather up inner edge of collar with gathering thread then pin collar to edge of neck rib, starting and finishing half way across the front bands. Stitch in place (**Diagram 2** see page 94). Sew on buttons to correspond to buttonholes.

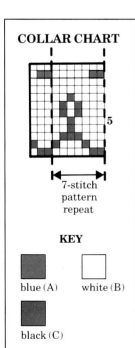

COLLAR CHART

5

7-stitch
pattern
repeat

KEY

blue (A)   white (B)

black (C)

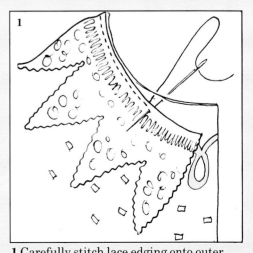

1 Carefully stitch lace edging onto outer edge of collar.

Version 2: for evening — a pink silk cardigan with decorative collar and cuffs shimmering with rhinestones and pearls.

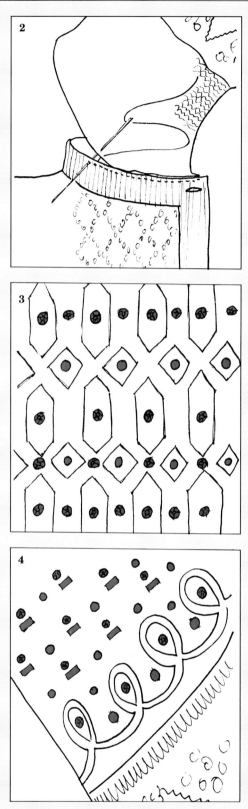

2 Stitch collar to edge of neck rib. **3** Version 2: decorate main pieces with pearls and rhinestones. **4** Version 2: decorate collar with pearls and rhinestones.

VERSION 2

PINK BEADED LACE CARDIGAN WITH LACE COLLAR AND CUFFS

MATERIALS
Yarn
Use double-knit weight.
625 (650 : 675)g/22(23 : 24)oz pink silk (A), 125g (5oz) white cotton (B)
Needles, other materials and tension as for Version 1.
For decoration
500 small pearls
100 clear rhinestones
100 pink rhinestones
100 blue rhinestones

METHOD
Work the back, front, sleeves, lace cuffs and bands as for Version 1.
Follow the stay stitching instructions, but do not sew pieces together or work neckband.
On the collar work A for B for main background colour, and work B for C and A in Fair Isle patterning – this means that the collar is in pink silk with white pattern.
Work collar edging as for Version 1.

DECORATION
This should be done before the garment is sewn up. It is easier to sew beads onto the flat pieces.
Decorate main pieces **(Diagram 3).**
Decorate collar **(Diagram 4).**
Follow all other making up instruction as for Version 1.

VERSION 3

WHITE LACE CARDIGAN WITH PLAIN RIBBED NECK AND CUFFS.

MATERIALS
Yarn
Use double-knit weight.
625 (650 : 675)g/22(23 : 24)oz white (A)
Needles and other materials
1 pair each of 3¼mm (US 10) and 4mm (US 6) needles
8 buttons
2 safety pins
Tension as for Version 1.

METHOD
Work back and fronts as for Version 1.

SLEEVES
Make 2. With 3¼mm needles and A, cast on 42 sts and work in K1, P1 rib for 2.5cm (1in).
Increase row: Rib and inc 43 sts evenly across row – 85 sts.
Change to 4mm needles and work in pattern and shaping as for Version 1.
Omit lace cuffs, collar and collar edging.
Follow all other instructions for making up, front bands, neckband etc.

Version 3: a plain white lace cardigan.

BROCADE WAISTCOAT

MEASUREMENTS (see also page 170)

Three sizes	small	medium	large
To fit bust:	81-86cm (32-34in)	91-97cm (36-38in)	102-107cm (40-42in)
Actual measurement (omitting borders):	98cm (38½in)	105cm (41¼in)	113cm (44½in)
Length from shoulder (omitting bottom edging):	49cm (19¼in)	49cm (19¼in)	49cm (19¼in)

VERSION 1

MATERIALS
Yarn
100(125 : 150)g/4(5 : 6)oz black Aran (A), 100(100 : 125)g/4(4 : 5)oz pink mohair (B), 100(125 : 125)g/4(5 : 5))oz white cotton DK (C), 75g(3oz) black cotton 4-ply (D)
Needles
1 pair each of 4½mm (US 7) and 6mm (US 10) needles

Tension
18 sts and 17 rows to 10cm (4in) on 6mm needles and main Fair Isle pattern.

> **NOTE**
> ● When working from chart weave in yarns on wrong side of work over not more than 3 sts at a time to keep fabric elastic.

BACK
With 6mm needles and A, cast on 94(100 : 106) sts and starting with a K row work in st st from chart between appropriate lines for size required until row 34 has been worked.

Shape armholes
Cast off 8 sts at beg of next 2 rows – 78(84 : 90)sts.
Now dec 1 st at each end of next row and every foll alt row until 70(76 : 82)sts remain.
Now cont straight following chart until row 84 has been worked.

Shape shoulders
Cast off 6(7 : 8) sts at beg of next 6 rows.
Cast off rem 34 sts for back neck.

RIGHT FRONT
With 6mm needles and A, cast on 42(45 : 48)sts and work between appropriate lines for right front on chart until row 35 has been worked.

Shape armhole
Cast off 8 sts at beg of row.
Now dec 1 st at armhole edge on next row and every foll alt row until 30(33 : 36)sts remain.
Now cont straight following chart until row 76 has been worked.

Shape front neck
Cast off 6 sts, patt to end – 24(27 : 30)sts.
Now dec 1 st on neck edge on every row until 18(21 : 24)sts remain. Cont straight following chart until row 85 has been worked.

Shape shoulder
Cast off 6(7 : 8)sts at beg of next row and 2 foll alt rows.

LEFT FRONT
Work as for right front but following chart for left front, working shapings on rows as indicated.

TO MAKE UP
Sew in all ends and gently press pieces on wrong side of work. Join shoulder seams.

Armhole edgings
Alike. With 4½mm needles and C and with RS facing, pick up and K 80 sts around one armhole edge. Work in K1, P1 rib in C for 6 rows.
Now using C and D together, work a picot cast-off edge as follows:
* Cast on 3 sts, cast off 5 sts, slip the stitch rem on RH needle back onto LH needle and rep from * to end. Join side seams and armhole edgings.

Bottom edging
With 4½mm needles and C and RS facing, pick up and K 38(40 : 42)sts along bottom edge of front, 90(92 : 94)sts at back and 38(40 : 42)sts along other front edge – 166(172 : 178)sts.
Starting with a P row work 3 rows in st st in C.
Next row: (RS facing) *K3C, K1D, rep from * to last 2(0 : 2)sts, K2(0 : 2)C. Work 3 more rows in st st in C. Now work the picot cast-off edge in C and D tog as for armhole.

Front bands
Alike. With 4½mm needles and C and RS facing, pick up and K 60 sts evenly along one front edge (including edge of bottom edging) and work to match bottom edging, working pattern row as for medium size.

Neck edging
With 4½mm needles and C and RS facing, pick up and K 20 sts along front neck (including edge of front band), 28 sts at back neck and 20 sts along other front neck and band – 68 sts. Work in K1, P1 rib in C for 5 rows. Work picot cast-off edge in C and D as before. *Other versions on page 164.*

WAISTCOAT CHART

KEY

black (A)   pink (B)

back neck – 34 stitches

89

85

75

65

55

45

35

25

15

5

1st size – 94 stitches

2nd size – 100 stitches

3rd size – 106 stitches

right front   left front

Version 2: the colours of the brocade-pattern waistcoat change to blue and black with black rib edging.

Version 3: plain black mohair waistcoat with a black and white picot border.

18th CENTURY INTRODUCTION

Eighteenth-century costume has characteristics that today we consider to be essentially feminine elements of dress: flowing shapes in softly coloured fine silks, often embroidered and trimmed with lace and ribbons, braid, feathers, artificial and even real flowers. Contemporary society provided a fit setting for such decorative and frivolous clothes. The rich and aristocratic met in gilded salons or Adam drawing-rooms, listened to the music of the harpsichord and spinet, and cultivated an atmosphere of light romance typified by the paintings of Fragonard.

The spirit of the century found fullest expression in France. Fashion in all the capitals of Europe was dictated by Paris and the court of Louis XV, whose long reign spanned almost sixty years, from 1715 to 1774. Louis XV could only echo the magnificence of his predecessor, the 'Sun King', and it is perhaps indicative of the time that life at his Versailles court centred on the personality of a woman, his mistress, Madame de Pompadour.

A pretty bourgeois Parisienne elevated by her relationship with the King, Madame de Pompadour was often painted by the leading court painter of the day, François Boucher. The portraits depict her dresses with exquisite detail, and these have provided a source of inspiration for the 18th-Century Sweater (see photograph, page 113).

The most elegant and expensive dresses to be found at Versailles, Madame de Pompadour's were made from the finest silks, richly embroidered, often with gold or silver thread or with floral designs. The bodice of each dress was usually cut low and square, and split at the front – like the sweater – to reveal a decorative panel called the 'stomacher', which was made from a contrasting fabric, and decorated with lace or ruching or sometimes with tiers of ribbons tied into bows. Bodice and stomacher were trimmed with *passementerie* – strips of gold or silver lace or braid, sometimes shaped into artificial flowers. The sleeves were elbow-length, usually finished with ribboned frills or ruching and worn with deep lace cuffs. The skirt, like the bodice, was split at the front, and beneath it was worn an embroidered or quilted petticoat supported by side hoops or 'panniers', a fashion some women took to enormous extremes. Madame de Pompadour

Rococo silk design of naturalistic swirling flowers by late eighteenth-century textile designer William Kilburn.

often wore a ribboned choker around her neck to match the dress, and a spray of flowers in her hair.

Men's clothing, also well recorded in the portraits of Boucher and others, was only slightly more restrained than that of women. Noblemen in curled and powdered wigs are shown in frock coats made from colourful silks and velvets, often trimmed with gold or silver ribbon braid. The coats usually had a small, stand-up collar and deep, fan-shaped cuffs, which were sometimes decorated with buttons to match those down the front of the coat and on the two pockets.

The white lace cuffs of an undershirt protruded beneath these wide 'boot-cuffs', as they were called. Coats were always worn open at the front to display a long waistcoat made from rich brocaded or embroidered silk for formal wear. At the neck was a cravat of linen or muslin, trimmed with lace, or from about 1749 onwards, a stock – a length of muslin wound round the neck and knotted in front, usually with the ends tucked in. The ensemble was worn over tight knee breeches. It was an elegant and flattering style, of which the 18th-Century Jacket and 18th-Century Waistcoat in this chapter give a taste (see photograph, page 103).

This fine clothing, for all its many layers and delicate trimmings, was looser and less formal than the styles of the previous century, and reflected a move towards greater naturalness in the eighteenth-century outlook. Intellectually, the idea was developed by writers and thinkers such as Rousseau, who believed in the beauty and innocence of nature and of the pastoral existence. But before Rousseau gave serious substance to the idea, artists such as Watteau, Lancret and of course Boucher painted romanticized scenes of rural life.

In the first half of the eighteenth century architects and decorative artists took motifs from nature, incorporating flowing lines and leafy decorations into Rococo ornamentation of buildings and of lavishly gilded Louis XV furniture, and into the patterns of fabrics and embroidery.

Flowers, birds and shells were favourite embroidery subjects, and there was a vogue for naturalistic botanical designs on fabrics, particularly during the middle years of the century. The Rococo-style floral pattern knitted in this cotton and silk sweater, over-embroidered in a darker thread to suggest swirling flower stems, takes its theme from the silk brocades of this period.

Painters liked to suggest that the beribboned dresses of the ladies, with their floral decoration and clear pastel colours, imitated the attire of delicate Arcadian shepherdesses. It was fashionable to extol the beauty of simple rural pursuits. Yet, when Madame de Pompadour and Louis XV took a few members of their huge entourage to what they called a 'hermitage', or rural retreat, they merely exchanged a palace for a stately mansion. This artificial pastoralism was taken to an extreme later in the century by Marie Antoinette, the wife of Louis XV's grandson and successor, Louis XVI. The story is often told – perhaps unfairly – of how she, arrogant and frivolous, played at being a milkmaid, churning butter in her toy farm at Versailles, careless of the harsh reality of life beyond the palace gates. Beneath the decorative veneer of the age, strong currents were flowing, which broke to the surface with the French Revolution in 1789.

Madame de Pompadour *painted by François Boucher in 1759, wearing a typical lace and bow-trimmed confection.*

18th CENTURY JACKET

MEASUREMENTS (see also page 170)

Three sizes	small	medium	large
To fit bust:	81-86cm (32-34in)	91-97cm (36-38in)	102-112cm (40-44in)
Actual measurement:	100cm (39¼in)	109cm (43in)	118cm (46½in)
Length from shoulder:	73cm (28¾in)	76cm (30in)	79cm (31in)
Sleeve seam (without lace cuff):	38cm (15in)	41cm (16¼in)	44cm (17¼in)

VERSION 1

MATERIALS

Yarn

Use double-knit weight: 150(150 : 175)g/6(6 : 7)oz white cotton (A), 675(700 : 725)g/24(25 : 26)oz multi-coloured cotton slub (B)

Needles and other materials

1 pair each of 3¾mm (US 4) and 4½mm (US 7) needles
8 buttons
Spare needles

For decoration

6 matching buttons
8 metres (9 yds) of 5mm (¼in) wide gold ribbon
8 metres (9 yds) of matching coloured cord
4.5 metres (5 yds) of flower braid
2 × 75cm (29½in) of 10cm (4in) wide lace
Shirring elastic
Gold lurex for embroidery
Embroidery needle

Tension

18 sts and 25 rows to 10cm (4in) on 4½mm needles and st st.

NOTES

- Any double-knit weight yarn can be used whether silk, cotton or wool as long as the tension is the same as that given.

- When working in more than one colour, twist yarns around each other on wrong side at joins to avoid making holes.

BACK

(Worked in two halves)

Left side

With 4½mm needles and A, cast on 50(54 : 58)sts and work in K1, P1 rib for 2 rows.
Now starting with a K row, work 16 rows in st st in A.
Next row: (RS facing) K10A, K40(44 : 48)B.
Next row: P40(44 : 48)B, P10A.
Rep these 2 rows until back measures 19(21.5 : 24)cm/7½(8½ : 9½)in from cast-on edge, ending with a WS row.
Break off A. Work 4 rows in st st in B only.

Decrease for waist:

Next row: (RS facing) Dec 17(18 : 19)sts evenly across row – 33(36 : 39)sts. Work 5 rows in st st.
Increase row: (RS facing) Inc 1 st in every 3rd st of row – 44(48 : 52)sts.
Cont straight in st st on these sts until back measures 48(51 : 54)cm/19(20 : 21¼)in from cast-on edge, ending with a RS row (side edge).

Shape armhole

Cast off 8 sts at beg of next row – 36(40 : 44)sts.
Dec 1 st at armhole edge on every alt row until 33(37 : 41)sts remain.
Now cont straight in st st until back measures 73(76 : 79)cm/28¾(30 : 31)in from cast-on edge, ending at armhole edge.

Shape shoulder

Cast off 6(7 : 8)sts at beg of next row and foll 2 alt rows.
Cast off rem 15(16 : 17)sts for half of back neck.

Right side

With 4½mm needles and A, cast on 50(54 : 58)sts and work 2 rows in rib and 16 rows in st st as for left side.
Next row: (RS facing) K40(44 : 48)B, K10A.
Next row: P10A, P40(44 : 48)B.
Rep these 2 rows until right back measures the same as left back to waist shaping.
Now follow shaping instructions and work as for left back, but reverse all shapings for armhole and shoulder.

POCKET LININGS

Make 2. With 4½mm needles and B, cast on 24 sts and starting with a K row, work straight in st st in B for 12cm (4¾in) ending with a WS row. Leave sts on a spare needle.

RIGHT FRONT

With 4½mm needles and A, cast on 50(54 : 58)sts and work 2 rows in rib and 16 rows in st st as for left side back.
Next row: (RS facing) K10A, K40(44 : 48)B.
Next row: P40(44 : 48)B, P10A.
Rep these 2 rows until front measures 18cm (7in) from cast-on edge, ending with a WS row.

Place pocket lining

Next row: Patt 16(20 : 24)sts, slip next 24 sts onto a length of yarn to be worked later, and instead of these sts work across the 24 sts of one pocket lining, patt to end of row – 50(54 : 58)sts.
Now cont straight in patt as set until front measures the same as back to waist shaping, ending with a WS row.

Decrease for waist

Next row: K10A, now in B dec 1 st in every 4th st to end – 40(43 : 46)sts.
Next row: P30(33 : 36)B, P10A.
Next row: K10A, P30(33 : 36)B.
Next row: P30(33 : 36)B, P10A.
Increase row: (RS facing) K10A, inc 4(5 : 6)sts evenly across rest of sts – 44(48 : 52)sts.
Next row: P34(38 : 42)B, P10A.
Next row: K10A, K34(38 : 42)B.

opposite
Version 1: frock-coat style jacket in multi-coloured cotton slub trimmed with gold-highlighted flower braid and cording. Lavish lace trimming on the cuffs adds to the 'dandy' look. The jacket is worn over a pink silk waistcoat decorated with stripes of flowered braid.

Cont to rep the last 2 rows until front measures the same as back to armhole shaping ending at side edge.

**Shape armhole
Cast off 8 sts at beg of next row, patt to end – 36(40 : 44)sts.
Dec 1 st at armhole edge on every alt row until 33(37 : 41)sts remain.
Now cont straight in patt until front measures 66(69 : 72)cm/26(27¼ : 28¼)in from cast-on edge, ending at centre front.

Shape front neck
Cast off 10 sts at beg of next row, patt to end.
Dec 1 st at neck edge on every row until 18(21 : 24)sts remain. Now cont straight until front measures the same as back to shoulder shaping ending at armhole edge.

Shape shoulder
Cast off 6(7 : 8)sts at beg of next row and foll 2 alt rows.

LEFT FRONT
With 4½mm needles and A, cast on 50(54 : 58)sts and work 2 rows in rib and 16 rows in st st as for left side back.
Next row: (RS facing) K40(44 : 48)B, K10A.
Next row: P10A, P40(44 : 48)B.
Rep these 2 rows until front measures 18cm (7in) from cast-on edge, ending with a WS row.

Place pocket lining
Next row: Patt 10 sts, slip next 24 sts onto a length of yarn to be worked later, and instead of these sts work across the 24 sts of second pocket lining, patt 16(20 : 24)sts – 50(54 : 58)sts.
Now cont straight in patt as set until front measures the same as back to waist shaping, ending with a WS row.

Decrease for waist
Next row: In B dec 1 st in every 4th st to last 10 sts, K10A – 40(43 : 46)sts.
Work 3 rows in patt as set.
Increase row: (RS facing) Inc 4(5 : 6)sts evenly across the next 30(33 : 36)sts, K10A – 44(48 : 52)sts.
Next row: P10A, P34(38 : 42)B.
Next row: K34(38 : 42)B, K10A.
Cont to rep the last 2 rows until front measures the same as back to armhole shaping, ending at side edge.
Now work as for right front from **to end, but reversing all shapings.

SLEEVES
Make 2. With 4½mm needles and A, cast on 56 sts and starting with a K row, work 16 rows in st st.
Next row: (RS facing) K22B, K12A, K22B (use two separate balls of B).
Next row: P22B, P12A, P22B.
Rep these 2 rows until sleeve measures 12cm (4¾in) from cast-on edge, ending with a WS row.
Break off A.
K1 row in B.
Cont in st st in B and inc 1 st at each end of 2nd row and then every foll 3rd row until 90 sts are on the needle.
Now cont straight in st st until sleeve measures 38(41 : 44)cm/15(16¼ : 17¼)in from cast-on edge, ending with a WS row.

Shape top
Cast off 8 sts at beg of next 2 rows – 74 sts.
Dec 1 st at beg of next 18 rows.
Cast off rem 56 sts.

Sew in ends and press all pieces carefully.

POCKET TOPS
Alike. With 3¾mm needles and B and RS facing work in K1, P1 rib across the 24 sts of one pocket top for 10 rows, thus ending with a WS row.***
Change to 4½mm needles and P1 row (work is now reversed for pocket flap).
Next row: P in A for fold-line.
Next row: P in A.
Starting with a K row, work in st st in A for 10 rows.

Shape pocket flap
Work 2 tog at each end of every row until all sts are worked. Fasten off.

TO MAKE UP
Sew in ends.
Stitch edges of pocket linings lightly to inside of fronts. Stitch sides of pocket ribs lightly to outside. Press pockets.
Join centre back seam together leaving open bottom 17(19.5 : 22)cm/6¾(7¾ : 8¾)in for flap.
Join shoulder seams together.
Join top sleeve edges to armhole edges.

DECORATION
Decorate the white borders of cuffs, front edges, bottom edges etc, with gold ribbon, cord and flower braid stitched on by hand (**Diagram 1** see page 106 for diagrams).
The cord can either be bought in a matching colour or can be made up as shown in the instructions for the *Renaissance Sweater I* page 64, using matching colours of 4-ply yarn twisted together. For the jacket in the photograph 1 length of pink, 1 length of pale green and 2 lengths of gold lurex were worked together.
Decorate edges of pocket flaps with flower braid (**Diagram 2**).
Chain stitch gold leaf shapes in between flower braid (**Diagram 3**).
Join underarm and side seams.

Neckband
With 4½mm needles and A and RS facing, pick up and K 22 sts from centre front to shoulder seam, 26 sts at back neck and 22 sts to centre front – 70 sts.
P1 row in A.
Now starting with a K row, work in st st in A until collar measures 5cm (2in) ending with a K row.
Next row: (WS facing) K for fold-line.
Starting with a K row, work a further 5cm (2in) in st st in A (for facing of collar).
Cast off loosely.
Press collar. Decorate collar with ribbon, cord and flower braid to match white edges.
Fold collar in half to inside and slip stitch facing carefully into place (**Diagram 4**).

Button band
With 3¾mm needles and A, and RS facing, pick up and K 124(130 : 136)sts evenly along left front edge (not edge of collar).
Work 7 rows in K1, P1 rib in A.
Cast off fairly loosely in rib.

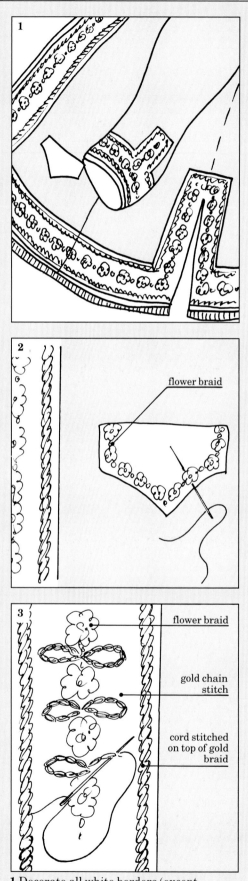

1 Decorate all white borders (except pockets) with gold ribbon, cord and flower braid. **2** Decorate edges of pocket flaps with flower braid. **3** Chain stitch gold leaf shapes between flowers on braid.

flower braid

gold chain stitch

cord stitched on top of gold braid

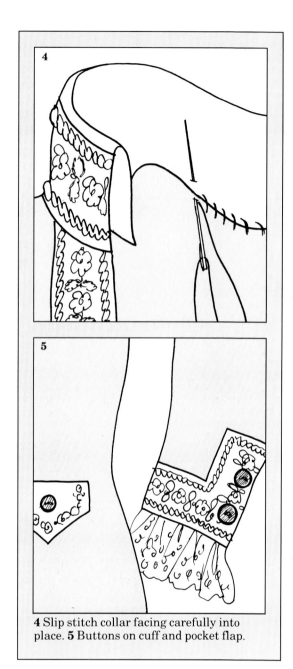

4 Slip stitch collar facing carefully into place. **5** Buttons on cuff and pocket flap.

Buttonhole band

Pick up sts along right front edge as for button band and work 3 rows in rib.

Next row: (RS facing - buttonhole row) Rib 12, *cast off 2 sts, rib 8 (including st on RH needle), cast off 2 sts, rib 20(22 : 24), rep from *twice more, cast off 2 sts, rib 8 (including st on RH needle), cast off 2 sts, rib 4.

Next row: Rib, casting on 2 sts over cast-off sts on previous row (8 buttonholes worked).

Work 2 more rows in rib.

Cast off fairly loosely in rib.

Lace cuffs

Alike. Take one length of lace and gather up one edge to fit cuff.

Join the ends of the lace together and carefully sew lace to inside of cuff.

Run a line of shirring elastic around back at decreased waistline to give garment more shape.

Sew on buttons to correspond with buttonholes.

Sew a button onto each pocket flap.

Sew 2 buttons onto each cuff (**Diagram 5**).

See page 165 for Versions 2 and 3 patterns.

Version 2: this jacket is knitted in a plain yarn with white contrast trim which is left undecorated.

Version 3: plain high-necked jacket knitted in a multi-coloured cotton slub throughout.
The back is knitted in one piece.

18th CENTURY WAISTCOAT

MEASUREMENTS (see also page 170)

Three sizes	small	medium	large
To fit bust:	81-86cm (32-34in)	86-91cm (34-36in)	91-97cm (36-38in)
Actual measurement:	91cm (36in)	97cm (38in)	102cm (40in)
Length from shoulder:	56cm (22in)	59cm (23¼in)	62cm (24½in)

VERSION 1

MATERIALS
Yarn
Use double-knit weight: 250(275 : 300)g/9(10 : 11)oz pink silk
Needles and other materials
1 pair each of 3¼mm (US 3) and 4mm (US 6) needles
5 buttons
For decoration
7 metres (7¾ yds) of 2cm (¾in) wide flower braid or ribbon

Tension
22 sts and 28 rows to 10cm (4in) on 4mm needles and st st.

> ### NOTE
> ● Any double-knit weight yarn can be used whether silk, cotton or wool, as long as the tension is the same as that given.

BACK
With 3¼mm needles cast on 100(106 : 112)sts and work in K1, P1 rib for 6 rows.
Change to 4mm needles and starting with a K row, work straight in st st until back measures 30(33 : 36)cm/11¾(13 :14¼)in from cast-on edge, ending with a WS row.

Shape armholes
Cast off 10 sts at beg of next 2 rows – 80(86 : 92)sts.
Dec 1 st at beg of next 8 rows – 72(78 : 84)sts.
Cont straight in st st until back measures 56(59 : 62)cm/22(23¼ : 24½)in from cast-on edge, ending with a WS row.

Shape shoulders
Cast off 7(8 : 9)sts at beg of next 6 rows.
Cast off rem 30 sts for back neck.

RIGHT FRONT
With 3¼mm needles cast on 50(52 : 56)sts and work in K1, P1 rib for 6 rows. *On middle size only,* inc 1 st on last row – 50(53 : 56)sts.
Change to 4mm needles and starting with a K row, work straight in st st until front measures 20(23 : 26)cm/8(9 : 10¼)in from cast-on edge, ending with a WS row.

Shape front slope
Dec 1 st at beg (neck edge) of next row and at this edge on every foll 6th row until front measures the same as back to armhole shaping, ending at side edge.

Shape armhole
Keeping dec at front edge as set, cast off 10 sts at beg of next row. Work 1 row.
Now dec 1 st at armhole edge on next row and 3 foll alt rows.
Cont straight at armhole edge and still dec at centre front as set until there are 21(24 : 27)sts on the needle.
Cont straight in st st on these sts until front measures the same as back to shoulder shaping, ending at armhole edge.

Shape shoulder
Cast off 7(8 : 9)sts at beg of next row and foll 2 alt rows.

LEFT FRONT
Work as for right front but reverse all shapings. Sew in ends and press pieces carefully according to ball band instructions.

DECORATION
The waistcoat may be decorated by stitching on flower braid (or ribbon) vertically on the fronts as follows:
(NB on the example given the flower braid is used with wrong side facing to give a chintz effect.)
Lay fronts on a flat surface and position strips of braid vertically at approx 1.5cm (½ in) intervals, leaving a 2.5cm (1in) overlap at each end for finishing off. Pin each strip carefully into position (**Diagram 1**, see page 110 for diagrams) – follow the vertical lines of the stitches for accuracy. You should be able to fit in 6 strips on each front on the smallest size. Make the intervals slightly wider between strips on larger sizes. Take care not to stretch the knitting when pinning and stitching on the braid. Machine stitch each strip into place neatly on either side using a matching colour thread (**Diagram 2**).
Fold the remaining overlap of each strip in half over to wrong side of work and neatly slip stitch down (**Diagram 3**).
Also slip stitch edges of braid down where they cross over shaped edges of fronts and armholes.
The back is not decorated
Join shoulder seams together.

ARMHOLE EDGINGS
Alike. With 3¼mm needles cast on 6 sts and work in K1, P1 rib until edging measures the same as armhole edge, when slightly stretched. Cast off ribwise. Join edgings to armholes.
Join side and edging seams.

LEFT FRONT BAND
With 3¼mm needles cast on 8 sts and work in K1, P1 rib until band measures up centre front edge to centre back neck, when slightly stretched.

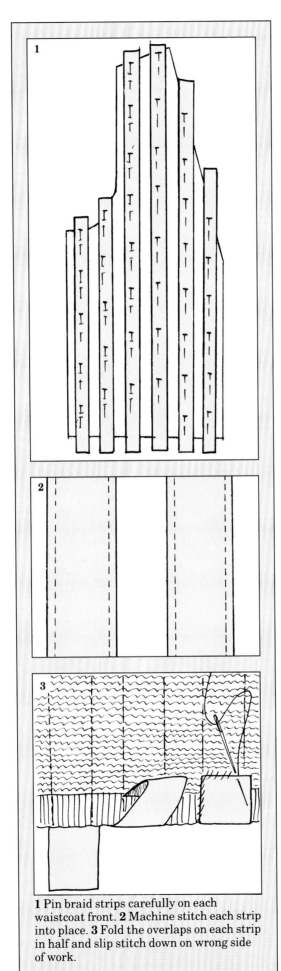

Carefully sew in position as you go along.
Cast off ribwise.
On this band mark positions for 5 buttons, the
first coming 2cm (¾in) up from cast-on edge, and
the remaining four at 6cm (2¼in) intervals.

RIGHT FRONT BAND
Work as for left front band but work buttonholes
to correspond to markers.
Buttonhole row: (RS facing) Rib 3, cast off 2 sts,
rib to end.
Next row: Rib, casting on 2 sts over cast-off sts
on previous row.
Complete as for left front band.

Join bands together at centre back neck.
Press all seams and bands carefully.
Sew on buttons to correspond with buttonholes.

VERSION 2

STRIPED WAISTCOAT

MATERIALS
Yarn
Use double-knit weight: 150 (175 : 175)g/6(7 : 7)oz
white cotton (A), 100 (100 : 125)g/4(4 : 5)oz silk in
colour of choice (B)
Needles and tension as for Version 1.

METHOD
Work as for Version 1.
The welts, armhole edgings and front bands are
knitted in white, but the body is knitted
throughout in st st in stripes of any combination
of rows, i.e: 2 rows, 4 rows or 8 rows of each
colour. Follow pattern using stripe sequence
chosen. Complete as for Version 1 but omit the
decoration.

VERSION 3

PLAIN WAISTCOAT

MATERIALS
Yarn
Use double-knit weight: 250(275 : 300)g/
9(10 : 11)oz yarn of choice
Needles and tension as for Version 1.

METHOD
Follow pattern for Version 1 but omit all
decoration.

1 Pin braid strips carefully on each
waistcoat front. **2** Machine stitch each strip
into place. **3** Fold the overlaps on each strip
in half and slip stitch down on wrong side
of work.

Versions 2 and 3 of the waistcoat: Version 2 can be knitted in stripes of different widths while Version 3 is completely plain.

18th CENTURY SWEATER

MEASUREMENTS (see also page 170)

Three sizes	small	medium	large
To fit bust:	81-86cm (32-34in)	91-97cm (36-38in)	102cm (40in)
Actual measurement:	95cm (37½in)	100cm (39½in)	106cm (41¾in)
Length from shoulder:	59cm (23¼in)	59cm (23¼in)	59cm (23¼in)
Sleeve seam:	28cm (11in)	28cm (11in)	28cm (11in)

VERSION 1

MATERIALS
Yarn
Use double-knit weight: 250(275 : 300)g/9(10 : 11)oz pale blue cotton (A), 100(100 : 125)g/4(4 : 5)oz pink silk (B), 200(225 : 225)g/8(8 : 8)oz yellow cotton (C), 100(100 : 125)g/4(4 : 5)oz white cotton (D), 50(75 : 75)g/2(3 : 3)oz green silk (E), 50(75 : 75)g/2(3 : 3)oz blue silk in a darker shade (F) than the pale blue background colour
Needles
1 pair each of 3¼mm (US 3) and 4mm (US 6) needles
For decoration
1 metre (1¼ yds) flower braid
Embroidery needle

Tension
22 sts and 26 rows to 10cm (4in) on 4mm needles and flower pattern

> **NOTES**
> ● Any double-knit weight yarn can be used whether silk, cotton or wool as long as the tension is the same as that given.
>
> ● When working the flower motifs, wind off small amounts of the required colours so that each motif can be worked separately, twisting yarns around each other on wrong side at joins to avoid holes, and where necessary stranding yarn loosely across wrong side of work over not more than 3 sts at a time to keep fabric elastic.

BACK
With 3¼mm needles and A, cast on 84(90 : 96)sts and work in K1, P1 rib for 7cm (3in).
Increase row: Rib and inc 20 sts evenly across row – 104(110 : 116)sts. **
Change to 4mm needles and work in st st from **Chart for back** (see page 114), working between appropriate lines for size required until row 70 has been worked.

Shape armholes
Cast off 8 sts at beg of next 2 rows.
Now dec 1 st at each end of next row and foll 3 alt rows – 80(86 : 92)sts.
Cont straight following chart until row 134 has been worked.

Shape shoulders
Cast off 7(8 : 9)sts at beg of next 6 rows.
Cast off rem 38 sts for back neck.

FRONT
Work as for back to **.
Change to 4mm needles and work in st st from **Chart for front** (see page 115), working between appropriate lines for size required and noting centre panel of 38 sts is worked in F only.
Cont straight following chart until row 70 has been worked.

Shape armholes
Cast off 8 sts at beg of next 2 rows.
Now dec 1 st at each end of next row and foll 3 alt rows – 80(86 : 92)sts.
Cont straight following chart until row 102 has been worked.

Shape front neck
Next row: (Row 103) Patt 21(24 : 27)sts, cast off centre 38 sts and patt to end of row and cont on this last set of sts only.
Cont straight following chart until row 135 has been worked.

Shape shoulder
Cast off 7(8 : 9)sts at beg of next row, and 2 foll alt rows.
With WS facing rejoin yarn to neck edge of rem sts and work straight following chart until row 134 has been worked.
Shape shoulder as for other side.

SLEEVES
Make 2. With 3¼mm needles and A, cast on 44 sts and work in K1, P1 rib for 2.5cm (1in).
Increase row: Rib and inc 1 st in every st across row – 88 sts.
Change to 4mm needles and work in st st from **Chart for sleeve** (see page 116), increasing 1 st at each end of 4th row and then every foll 3rd row until there are 130 sts on the needle.
Work 2 rows straight ending with row 66 of chart.

Shape top
Cast off 8 sts at beg of next 2 rows.
Now dec 1 st at each end of every row until 56 sts remain.
Cast off.

TO MAKE UP
Sew in all ends and press pieces carefully on the wrong side.

DECORATION
Using F and working in a neat embroidery stitch – chain stitch, or back stitch – work stems and scrolls between flowers and leaf motifs (**Diagram 1** see page 116) – follow fine line on charts. Join right shoulder seam.

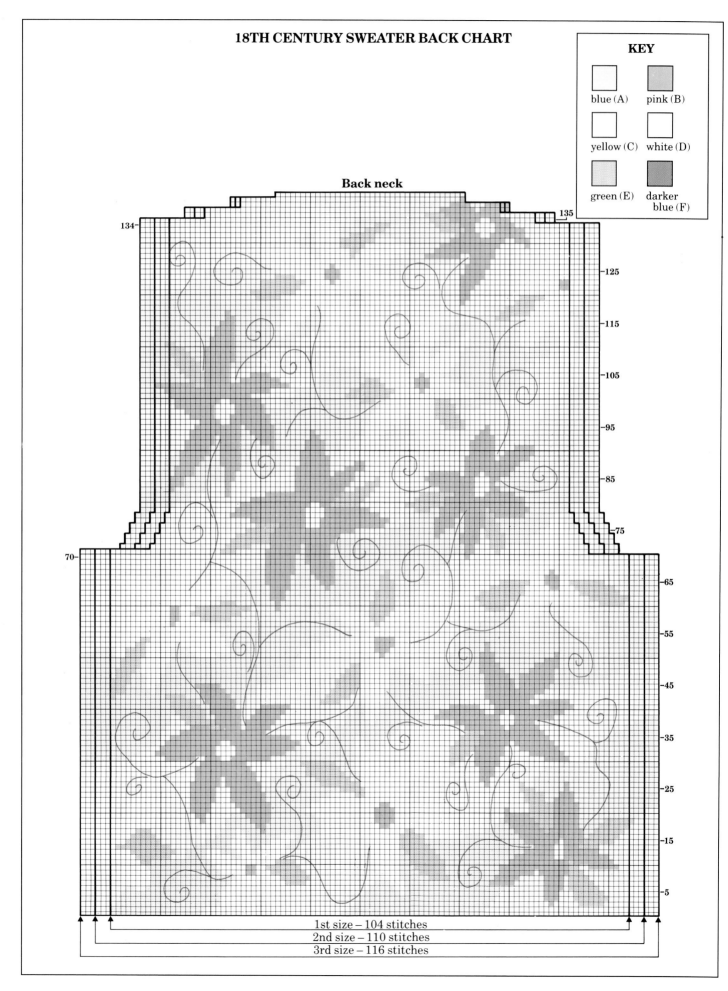

18TH CENTURY SWEATER BACK CHART

KEY

blue (A)   pink (B)

yellow (C)   white (D)

green (E)   darker blue (F)

Back neck

134 —

— 135

— 125

— 115

— 105

— 95

— 85

— 75

70 —

— 65

— 55

— 45

— 35

— 25

— 15

— 5

1st size – 104 stitches
2nd size – 110 stitches
3rd size – 116 stitches

18TH CENTURY SWEATER FRONT CHART

(see opposite for key)

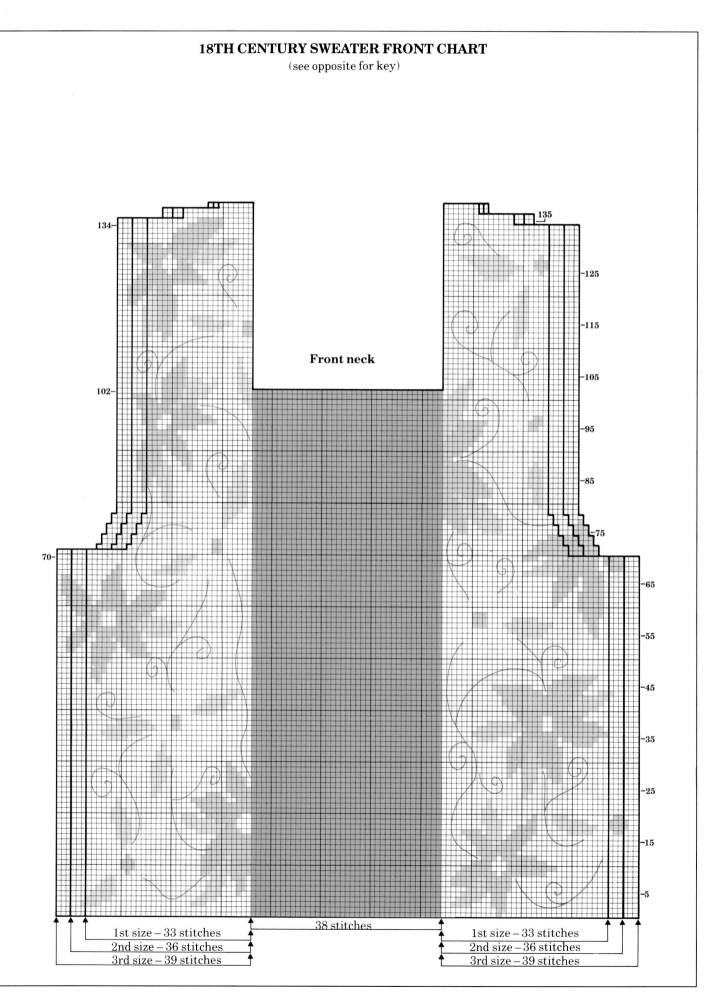

Front neck

134-
102-
70-

-135
-125
-115
-105
-95
-85
-75
-65
-55
-45
-35
-25
-15
-5

1st size – 33 stitches
2nd size – 36 stitches
3rd size – 39 stitches

38 stitches

1st size – 33 stitches
2nd size – 36 stitches
3rd size – 39 stitches

18TH CENTURY SWEATER SLEEVE CHART

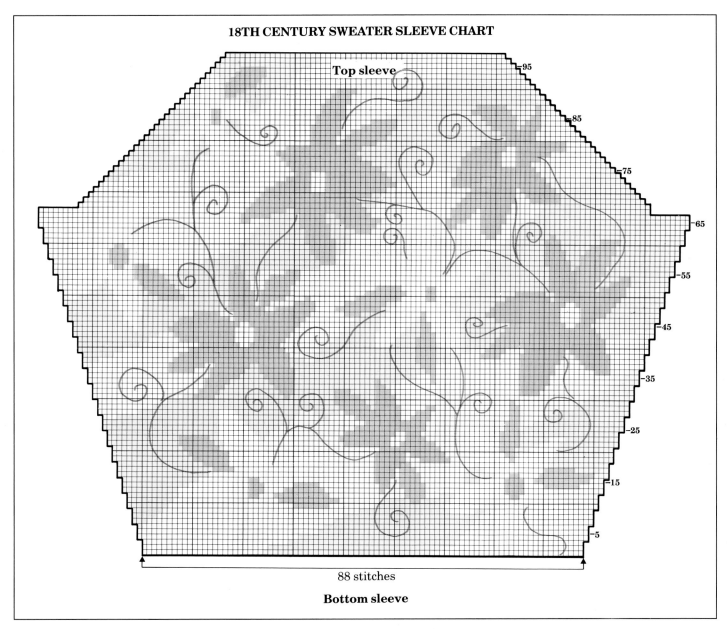

Top sleeve

—95
—85
—75
—65
—55
—45
—35
—25
—15
—5

88 stitches

Bottom sleeve

KEY

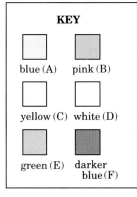

blue (A)   pink (B)

yellow (C)   white (D)

green (E)   darker blue (F)

1 Embroider stems and scrolls between flowers and leaf motifs in chain stitch or back stitch.

Neck ribbing

With 3¼mm needles and A, and RS facing, pick up and K 26 sts down left side neck, 1 corner st, 30 sts at front neck, 1 corner st, and 26 sts up other side of neck and 30 sts across back neck – 114 sts. Work in K1, P1 rib until 2 sts before corner st, then rib 2 tog, rib 1, rib 2 tog tbl. Repeat on other corner.

Work a further 5 rows in rib, dec at each corner as before. Cast off ribwise.

Join left shoulder and neck ribbing seam.

Gather up sleeve top with a gathering thread and adjust to fit armhole.

Place most of gathers over shoulder area, pin and sew sleeves into armholes.

Join underarm and side seams.

Press garment carefully.

Decorate front panel

By hand, stitch a strip of flower braid on each side of front where the plain panel joins the flower pattern (**Diagram 2**).

Bows

With 4mm needles and B, cast on 18 sts and work straight in K1, P1 rib for 12cm (5in). Cast off ribwise.

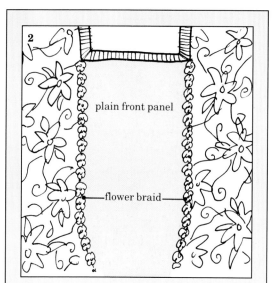

plain front panel

—flower braid—

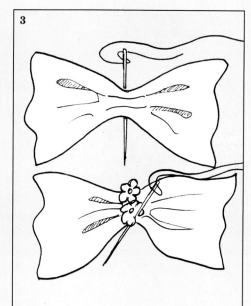

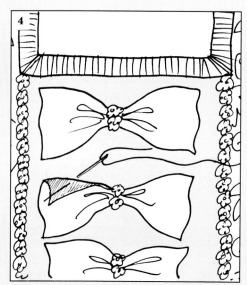

2 Stitch a strip of flower braid on either side of the centre panel. **3** Stitch a 4cm(1½in) length of flower braid around the middle of each bow. **4** Lightly stitch centre and each side of bows to centre panel to hold in place.

Work another bow in B.
Work 2 more bows each in C and E (6 bows worked in all).
Sew in ends and press lightly.
Form into bow shape by gathering up at centre and stitching together. Then cut a 4cm (1½in) length of flower braid and stitch around centre of bow **(Diagram 3)**.
Sew bows onto the centre panel of the sweater alternating the colours. Lightly stitch at centre and also at each side of the bows (to hold bows in place – **Diagram 4**).

VERSION 2

FLOWERED SWEATER WITHOUT DECORATION

MATERIALS
Yarn
Use double-knit weight: 100 (100 : 125)g/4 (4 : 5) oz pale blue cotton (A), 75 (75 : 100)g/3 (3 : 4)oz pink silk (B), 450 (475 : 500)g/16 (17: 18)oz white cotton (C), 100 (125 : 150)g/4 (5 : 6)oz green silk (D)
Needles and tension as for Version 1.

METHOD
The basic pattern is as for Version 1, but the colours are arranged differently so that the ribs and background colour are worked in white (C), the front panel is in green (D) and the flowers are in pale blue (A) and pink (B).
For yarns A and C in the original pattern work C above.
For yarns E and F in the original pattern work D above
For yarn D in the original pattern work A above. B remains the same.
Follow all instructions for making up but omit the embroidered decoration, flower braid and knitted bows.

VERSION 3

SWEATER KNITTED IN COLOUR BLOCKS WITHOUT DECORATION

MATERIALS
Yarn
Use double-knit weight: 175(200 : 225)g/7(8 : 8)oz pale blue cotton (A), 200(225 : 250)g/8(8 : 9)oz pink silk (B), 75g(3oz) yellow cotton (C), 75g(3oz) white cotton (D), 100g (4oz) green silk (E)
Needles and tension as for Version 1.

METHOD
This is a very simple version using the basic shape but working the whole garment in large blocks of colour.
Follow the instructions for Version 1 and work from charts following all shapings, but work colours as follows:

Welts: in pale blue (A).
Back: in pink (B).
Front: left side in white (D),
centre in pink (B) and right side
in yellow (C).
Right sleeve: in pale blue (A).
Left sleeve: in green (E).
Neck ribbing: in green (E).
Omit all decoration.

Version 2: the sweater features pink and blue flowers on a white background.
The green centre panel is undecorated.

Version 3: the basic pattern is translated into a modern style knitted in blocks of pastel colours.

VICTORIAN

INTRODUCTION

The sailor jacket and bobble sweater in this chapter are inspired by the styles of a specific decade of the Victorian era: the 1890s. The last years of the nineteenth century were the first time that a practical form of dress was available to active women, whether for working or sports.

Prior to the 1880s there was no special outfit for working women, although they had already begun to take non-domestic employment in growing numbers: in England the number of female shop assistants had reached 20,000 by 1871 and there were 18,000 women clerks by 1891. Fashion was still decreed by the primarily decorative role of leisured women, the very impracticality of whose clothes was intended to show that they were supported by well-to-do men, whether husband or father, and therefore did not need to work. Even 'emancipated' women active in public life were still constrained by the cumbersome crinolines and tight stays imposed by convention.

The great advance of the 1880s was the introduction of the tailored suit, said to have been pioneered by Creed or Redfern, both famous London couturiers. This outfit consisted of a gored skirt, often bias-cut, and fitted jacket, worn with either a plain shirt, starched collar and mannish tie, or a frilly blouse. The suit was made in serge or tweed for winter, linen for summer.

The need for and acceptance of this more 'modern'and practical style originated, however, not so much from working women themselves, nor even from the activists of the various dress reform movements then current, but rather from the invention of the 'safety bicycle'. Cycling quickly became a fashionable craze which reached its peak in the mid-1890s, when parks were thronged with debutantes and society ladies cycling up and down, wearing the bloomers championed by Amelia Bloomer in the United States in the 1850s, but not accepted until forty years later. Plain flared or divided skirts were worn too, and teamed

A French velveteen suit of jacket and Turkish trousers was perfect for bicycling in 1894.

with white tailored shirts formed an accepted dress for sport, in which girls and young women increasingly took part – tennis, hockey and golf were all popular.

As skirts became simpler and narrower after the demise of the crinoline, the upper half of the body became the focus of visual interest. Above the fashionable wasp waist jackets often had large lapels, sometimes giving a cape-like effect, and the width of sleeves expanded enormously, in a revival of a fashion current in the 1830s. Narrow from wrist to elbow, they ballooned out from elbow to shoulder in a large puff, giving rise to the name 'leg of mutton' or 'gigot' sleeves, a style which was at its most exaggerated from 1894-5. Both Sue Bradley's Victorian designs feature this look, with wide sleeves caught into long, narrow cuffs. In the 1890s short capes and mantles were worn as outerwear, probably because they could easily accommodate the bulkiness of the upper arm.

The bobble Victorian Sweater (see photograph, page 130) is inspired by the blouses of this period, with its full sleeves and small stand-up collar, worn with a knitted bow tie. The horizontal openwork bands knitted in silky white cotton yarn recall the rows of fine tucking or bands of lace with which blouses of the '90s were often decorated. (Although a severe tailored blouse was often worn in the daytime for work or sport, evening blouses were often in silk and elaborately decorated with lace and embroidery to compensate for the relative plainness of the skirt.) The bright blue and red are also in keeping: the late Victorians were fond of strong contrasting colours both for clothes and in popular art forms, such as the cheerful posters for music hall stars.

The breezy nautical look of the navy blue, white and red Victorian Sailor Jacket (see photograph, page 123), with its big sailor collar and frog fastening, was very popular in the latter half of the nineteenth century. As the expansion of the railway system made travel easier, more and more people spent restorative holidays by or on the sea. Since the Victorians deemed it essential to have correct – and different – clothes for every conceivable occasion, seaside and yachting clothes evolved for men, women and children which were highly elegant if not very practical for playing on the beach or actually going on board yachts.

Sailor suits for little boys were popular from the 1860s to the Edwardian period and consisted of knickerbockers and a blouse with a large square collar and V-shaped

front opening filled in with a striped vest or jersey. Girls had 'seaside dresses' in blue and white striped silk or cotton, again with the typical square collar, and often decorated with anchor motifs. With these outfits straw boaters or tam o'shanters were worn. Ladies' yachting costume was often a tailored suit in white linen or flannel with accessories and trimmings (often ribbon or braid) in navy blue. Again, anchors were a common decoration. Ladies also wore straw boaters, as in our picture, or might have favoured a nautical peaked cap to match their ensemble.

Late Victorian fashions show that by the end of the nineteenth century clothes specifically designed for leisure pursuits were being worn, foreshadowing what was to become a major fashion trend in the twentieth century.

The cover of an 1895 issue of the photographic journal, The Album, shows a young woman dressed in the fashion of the day – a nautical-style suit with leg of mutton sleeves worn with a white blouse and tie.

VICTORIAN SAILOR JACKET

MEASUREMENTS (see also page 171)

Three sizes	small	medium	large
To fit bust:	81-86cm (32-34in)	91-96cm (36-38in)	102-107cm (40-42in)
Actual measurement:	95cm (38in)	102cm (40in)	108cm (42½in)
Length from shoulder:	63cm (25in)	66cm (26in)	69cm (27in)
Sleeve seam:	43cm (17in)	46cm (18in)	48cm (19in)

VERSION 1

MATERIALS
Yarn
Use Aran weight: 675 (700 : 725)g/24 (25 : 26) oz navy wool (A), 50g (2oz) red wool (B), 150g (6oz) white cotton (C)
Needles and other materials
1 pair each of 4mm (US 6), 5mm (US 8) and 1 4mm (US 6) circular needle
Frogging fastener
2 large buttons
Shirring elastic

Tension
24 sts and 24 rows to 10cm (4in) on 5mm needles and rib patt without stretching

> ### NOTE
> • Any Aran-weight yarn can be used, as long as the tension is the same as that given above.

BACK
With 5mm needles and B, cast on 114 (122 : 130) sts and work in rib patt as follows:
**Row 1: (RS facing) With B, *K2, P6, rep from * to last 2 sts, K2.
Row 2: With B, *P2, K6, rep from * to last 2 sts, P2.
Row 3: K in A.
Row 4: With A, *P2, K6, rep from * to last 2 sts, P2.
Row 5: With A, *K2, P6, rep from * to last 2 sts, K2.
Rep the last 2 rows only until work measures 15cm (6in) from cast-on edge, ending with a WS row.**

Shape waist
Decrease row: With A, K1, *K2 tog, rep from * to last st, K1 – 58(62 : 66) sts.
Cont in A in double rib as follows:
Row 1: (WS facing) P2, *K2, P2, rep from * to the end.
Row 2: K2, *P2, K2, rep from * to end.
Rep the last 2 rows for 5cm (2in), ending with a WS row.
***Increase row: K1, *inc in next st, rep from * to last st, K1 – 114(122 : 130) sts.
Now work in rib patt as follows:
Row 1: *P2, K6, rep from * to last 2 sts, P2.
Row 2: *K2, P6, rep from * to last 2 sts, K2.
Rep the last 2 rows until back measures 35(38 : 41)cm/13¾ (15 : 16) in from cast-on edge, ending with a WS row.

Shape armholes
Keeping patt correct, cast off 10 sts at beg of next 2 rows – 94(102 : 110)sts.
Dec 1 st at beg of next 12 rows – 82(90 : 98) sts.
Cont straight in patt until back measures 63(66 : 69)cm/25(26 : 27) in from cast-on edge, ending with a WS row.

Shape shoulders
Cast off 8(9 : 10) sts at beg of next 6 rows.
Cast off rem 34(36 : 38) sts.

RIGHT FRONT
With 5mm needles and B, cast on 50(58 : 66) sts and work as for back from ** to **.

Shape waist
Decrease row: With A, K1, *K2 tog, rep from * to last st, K1 – 26 (30 : 34) sts.
Cont in A and work 5cm (2in) in double rib as for back, ending with a WS row.
Increase row: K1, *inc in next st, rep from * to last st, K1 – 50(58 : 66) sts.
Now work in rib patt as for back until front measures 23(25 : 28)cm/9(10 : 11)in from cast-on edge, ending with a WS row.

Shape neck
Dec 1 st at beg of next and every foll 6th row until front measures the same as back to start of armhole shaping, ending with a RS row.

Shape armhole
Cont to dec at neck edge on every 8th (6th : 4th) row from previous dec, cast off 10 sts at beg of next row then dec 1 st at armhole edge on 6 foll alt rows.
Keeping armhole edge straight, cont to dec at neck edge until 24(27 : 30) sts rem.
Now work a few rows straight in patt until front measures the same as back to start of shoulder shaping, ending at side edge.

Shape shoulder
Cast off 8(9 : 10) sts at beg of next and 2 foll alt rows.

LEFT FRONT
Work as for right front reversing all shapings.

Sleeves
Make 2. With 4mm needles and B, cast on 42 sts, work in stripe double rib as follows:
Row 1: (RS facing) With B, K2, *P2, K2, rep from * to end.
Row 2: With B, *K2, P2, rep from * to end.
Rows 3-10: With A, rep rows 1-2 4 times.
Rep last 10 rows until work measures 18cm (7in) from cast-on edge, ending with a WS row.

opposite
Version 1: jaunty nautical-style jacket knitted in a thick rib in navy blue Aran; it has a white cotton sailor collar and is trimmed in scarlet. The 'leg of mutton' sleeves, fitted waist and frogging fastener echo the fashions of the 1890s; the accessory is a navy knitted bow tie.

******Increase row:** With A, rib and inc in every st across row – 84 sts. Rep last row again – 168 sts.
Change to 5mm needles and cont in A only and rib patt as follows:
Row 1: (RS facing) *K2, P6, rep from * to end.
Row 2: *K6, P2, rep from * to end.
Rep the last 2 rows until sleeve measures 43(46 : 48)cm/17 (18 : 19) in from cast-on edge, ending with a WS row.

Shape top sleeve
Cast off 10 sts at beg of next 2 rows – 148 sts.
Dec 1 st at each end of every row until there are 100 sts rem.
Cast off.

TO MAKE UP
Sew in all ends.
Join shoulder seams. Gather top sleeve edge to fit armhole, arranging gathers evenly over shoulder. Sew in position. Join side and sleeve seams.

Collar
(Diagram 1), with 4mm circular needle, C and WS facing, starting above waist shaping on left front, pick up and K94 sts along front edge to shoulder, 40 sts from back neck and 94 sts along front edge to top of waist shaping on right front – 228 sts.
Next row: (RS facing) K for fold-line.
Work 2 rows in K2, P2 rib.

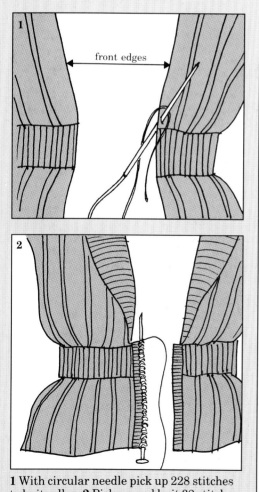

1 With circular needle pick up 228 stitches to knit collar. **2** Pick up and knit 32 stitches along front edge.

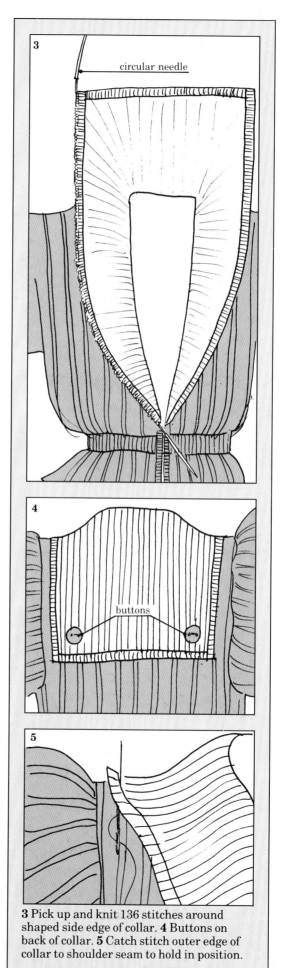

3 Pick up and knit 136 stitches around shaped side edge of collar. **4** Buttons on back of collar. **5** Catch stitch outer edge of collar to shoulder seam to hold in position.

*opposite
Version 1: back view of the jacket showing the sailor collar which is trimmed with two large buttons.*

Shape collar
Next row: Cast off 2 sts, rib to last 2 sts, K2 tog.
Rep the last row until 144 sts rem.*****
Cast off 38 sts at beg of next 2 rows – 68 sts.
Cont straight in rib until collar measures 28cm
(11in) from back neck edge, ending with a WS row.
Change to B.
Next row: K.
Work 2 rows in K2, P2 rib.
Cast off loosely in rib.

Centre front edgings
Alike (Diagram 2, see previous page for
diagrams).With 4mm needles and B, with RS
facing, pick up and K 32 sts along front edge
between cast-on edge and collar.
Work 2 rows K2, P2 rib.
Cast off in rib.

Collar edgings
Alike (Diagram 3). With 4mm circular needle
and B, with RS of collar facing, pick up and K136
sts along shaped side edge of collar.
Work 2 rows K2, P2 rib.
Cast off in rib.

If required, thread shirring elastic through
waist ribbing.
Stitch frogging fastener in position.
Sew buttons onto back of collar **(Diagram 4)**.
Catch stitch outer edge of collar to shoulder seam
to hold in position **(Diagram 5)**.

VERSION 2

STRIPED JACKET WITH SHAWL COLLAR

MATERIALS
Yarn
Use Aran weight: 375 (400 : 425)g/14 (15 : 15)oz
red wool (A), 175 (200 : 225)g/7 (8 : 8)oz navy wool
(B), 175 (200 : 225)g/7 (8 : 8)oz royal blue wool (C),
100g (4oz) white wool (D)
Needles and tension as Version 1.

BACK
With 5mm needles and B, cast on 114(122 : 130)
sts and work in rib patt as follows:
**Row 1: (RS facing) With B, *K2, P6, rep from *
to last 2 sts, K2.
Row 2: With B, *P2, K6, rep from * to last
2 sts, P2.
Rows 3-6: Rep rows 1–2 twice.
Rows 7-12: With A, rep rows 1-6.
Rows 13-18: With C, rep rows 1-6.
Rows 19-24: Rep rows 7-12.
Rows 25-36: Rep rows 1-12. **

Shape waist
Decrease row: With C, K1, *K2 tog, rep from *
to last st, K1 – 58(62 : 66) sts.
Cont in double rib as for back of Version 1, work 1
row in C, 2 rows A, 2 rows B, 2 rows A, 2 rows C, 2
rows A, 2 rows B, 2 rows A.
Complete as for Version 1 from *** to end,
working in stripe sequence of 6 rows C, 6 rows A,
6 rows B, 6 rows A throughout.

RIGHT FRONT
With 5mm needles and B, cast on 50(58 : 66) sts
and work as back of Version 2 from ** to **.
Complete as for right front of Version 1 working
in stripe sequence as given for back of Version 2.

LEFT FRONT
Work as for right front, reversing all shapings.

SLEEVES
Make 2. With 4mm needles and B, cast on 42 sts.
Cont in double rib as for cuff of sleeve of Version 1
working in stripe sequence of 2 rows B, 2 rows A,
2 rows C, 2 rows A until sleeve measures approx
18cm (7in) from cast-on edge ending with 2 rows B.

Complete as for sleeves of Version 1 from **** to
end, working in stripe sequence of 6 rows A, 6
rows B, 6 rows A, 6 rows C throughout.

TO MAKE UP
Work as for Version 1, omitting buttons.

Collar
Work as for Version 1 to *****. Cont in B only.
Next row: K.
Work 2 rows K2, P2 rib. Cast off in rib.

Centre front edgings
Work as for Version 1.

Collar edgings
Work as for Version 1, but pick up and K100 sts
in A along shaped edge of collar.

VERSION 3

JACKET IN ONE COLOUR ONLY WITH SHAWL COLLAR

MATERIALS
Yarn
Use Aran weight.
875 (900 : 925)g/31(32 : 33) oz of chosen colour
Needles and tension as Version 1.

METHOD
Work as for Version 2 in one colour only.

Version 2: the ribbed jacket is knitted in broad stripes of red, navy and royal blue. The white shawl collar is edged with navy.

Version 3: the jacket, knitted in one colour throughout, has the same shawl collar as Version 2 and is worn with a navy bow tie.

VICTORIAN SWEATER

MEASUREMENTS (see also page 171)

Three sizes	**small**	**medium**	**large**
To fit bust:	81-86cm (32-34in)	91-96cm (36-38in)	102-107cm (40-42in)
Actual measurement:	95cm (37½in)	103cm (40½in)	110cm (43½in)
Length from shoulder:	58cm (23in)	61cm (24in)	64cm (25in)
Sleeve seam:	43cm (17in)	46cm (18in)	48cm (19in)

VERSION 1

MATERIALS
Yarn
Use double-knit weight: 375(400 : 425)g/14 (15 : 15)oz royal blue wool (A), 200(225 : 250)g/8(8 : 9)oz white cotton (B), 75 (100 : 100)g/3 (4 : 4)oz red wool (C)

Needles
1 pair each of 3¼mm (US 3), 4mm (US 6) and 1 3¼mm (US 3) circular needle

Tension
21 sts and 26 rows to 10cm (4in) on 4mm needles and main patt.

NOTE
● Any double-knit weight can be used, as long as the tension is the same as that given above.

BACK
With 3¼mm needles and K, cast on 82 (90 : 98) sts and work in K1, P1 rib for 10cm (4in).
Increase row: Rib and inc 18 sts evenly across row – 100 (108 : 116) sts.
Change to 4mm needles and work in main patt as follows:
Row 1: (WS facing) K in A.
Row 2: K in A.
Row 3: K in B.
Row 4: K in B, wrapping yarn twice round the needle for each st.
Row 5: K in A dropping extra loops of the previous row.
Row 6: K in A.
Row 7: P in A.
Row 8: K in A.
Row 9: P in A.
Row 10: *K3A, in C(K1, P1, K1, P1) all into next st, slip 3rd, 2nd and 1st sts over 4th st, rep from * to end.
Row 11: P in A.
Row 12: K in A.
Rep last 12 rows until back measures 30 (33 : 36) cm/12(13 : 14)in from cast-on edge, ending with a WS row.

Shape armhole
Cast off 8 sts at beg of next 2 rows – 84(92 : 100)sts.
Dec 1 st at beg of next 8 rows – 76 (84 : 92) sts.
Now work straight in patt until back measures 58(61 : 63)cm/23(24 : 25)in from cast-on edge, ending with a WS row.

Shape shoulders
Cast off 7(8 : 9)sts at beg of next 6 rows.
Cast off rem 34(36 : 38) sts.

FRONT
Work as for back until front measures 14 rows less than back to start of shoulder shaping, ending with a WS row.

Shape neck
Next row: Patt 31(35 : 39)sts, cast off centre 14 sts, patt to end of row, and cont on this last set of sts only. **Dec 1 st at neck edge on every row until 21(24 : 27) sts rem.
Now work straight in patt until front measures the same as back to start of shoulder shaping, ending at side edge.

Shape shoulder
Cast off 7(8 : 9) sts at beg of next and 2 foll alt rows. With WS facing rejoin yarn to rem sts and work as for first side from ** to end.

SLEEVES
Make 2. With 3¼mm needles and A, cast on 48 sts and work in K1, P1 rib for 18cm (7in).
Increase row: Rib and inc in every st across row – 96 sts.
Change to 4mm needles and work in patt as for back, in 1 st at each end of every alt row until there are 152 sts.
Now work straight in patt until sleeve measures approx 43(46 : 48)cm/17(18 : 19) in from cast-on edge, ending with same patt row as back at start of armhole shaping.

Shape top sleeve
Cast off 8 sts at beg of next 2 rows – 136 sts.
Dec 1 st at beg of every row until 106 sts rem.
Cast off.

TO MAKE UP
Sew in all ends.
Join shoulder seams. Gather top sleeve to fit into armhole, arranging gathers evenly over shoulder. Sew in position. Join side and sleeve seams, matching patt.

Collar
Beg at centre of front neck sts, with 3¼mm circular needle and A, and RS facing, pick up and K6 sts from front neck, 22 sts along side of neck, 34 sts at back neck, 22 sts along side of neck and 6 sts from front neck – 90 sts.
Work 4 rounds in K1, P1 rib, ending at centre front. Now cont in rib as set, working in rows to form a split at centre front.
Cont in rib until collar measures 8cm(3in).
Cast off loosely in rib using a 4mm needle.

VERSION 2

WORKED IN STRIPES ONLY

MATERIALS
Yarn
Use double-knit weight: 475(500 : 525)g/17(18 : 19)oz navy blue wool (A), 200(225 : 250)g/8(8 : 9)oz white cotton (B)
Needles and tension as Version 1.

METHOD
This version is worked exactly as for Version 1, but work row 10 of patt on back as follows:
Row 10: K in A.

VERSION 3

WORKED IN ONE COLOUR ONLY

MATERIALS
Yarn
Use double-knit weight: 700(725 : 750)g/25(26 : 27)oz of chosen colour.
Needles and tension as for Version 1.

METHOD
Work as for Version 1 in one colour only.

VICTORIAN BOW TIE

MEASUREMENTS

To fit one size	
Approx width:	17cm(6½in)
Depth:	8.5cm(3¼in)

MATERIALS
Yarn
Use Aran weight.
15g (¾oz) wool or cotton
Needles and other materials
1 pair of 5mm (US 8) needles
Press-stud or hook and eye fastener

Tension
19 sts and 30 rows to 10cm (4in) on 5mm needles and patt.

> ### NOTES
> ● Any Aran-weight yarn can be used, whether cotton or wool, as long as the tension is the same as that given above.

METHOD
With 5mm needles cast on 16 sts. Work in moss st patt as follows:
Row 1: *K1, P1, rep from* to end.
Row 2: *P1, K1, rep from * to end.
Rep last 2 rows until work measures 17cm (6½in) from cast-on edge.
Cast off.

TIE
With 5mm needles cast on 3 sts and work in st st until tie is long enough to fit around neck and overlap by 1cm(½in).
Cast off

TO MAKE UP
Form centre of bow into pleats and stitch around with matching yarn (**Diagram 1**).
On WS stitch centre of tie to centre of bow (**Diagram 2**). Sew press-stud or hook and eye fastener to ends of tie.

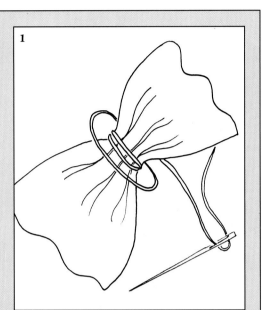

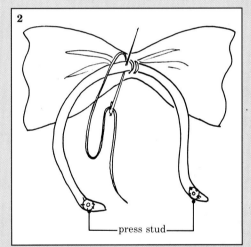

1 Form centre of bow into pleats and stitch around with matching yarn. **2** Stitch centre of tie to centre of bow.

opposite
Version 1: cheerful Victorian-style sweater worked in a bobble and lace stitch in red, white and blue has leg of mutton sleeves and a small stand-up collar. It is worn with a white knitted bow tie.

Version 2: there are no bobbles on this version – it is knitted in navy and lacy white stripes and teamed with a red bow tie.

Version 3: the bobble and lace stitch is knitted in all white for a sweater reminiscent of a late Victorian blouse.
It is worn with a blue bow tie.

THE TWENTIES
INTRODUCTION

The startling contrast between Edwardian women's clothes and those of the Twenties – one of the most radical changes of direction fashion has ever undergone – was largely due to the far-reaching effects on society of the First World War.

Impractical frills and furbelows were the hallmark of high Edwardian dress and the exaggerated curves of the fashionable figure relied on rigid corseting. Immediately before the war the line did become somewhat straighter, but fashions, such as the hobble skirt, were still constricting. The onset of war, disastrous in so many ways, actually had a liberating effect on women:

Beaded evening dress of silver chiffon and lace by Beer, 1922, illustrated by George Barbier in Gazette du Bon Ton.

withdrawal of male labour meant that women were working outside the home in far greater numbers than ever before. Their everyday clothes had therefore to become more practical: easier to wear and care for. In addition, there was a shortage of the luxury materials and skilled labour that had produced the extravagant fashions of the pre-war years. Inevitably, both during and after the war, styles became simpler, more comfortable and more economical in their use of fabric.

The most obvious development in the war years was the raising of the hemline, but although we think of the archetypal Twenties flapper in a knee-length shift, in fact hemlines fluctuated considerably. During the war they rose, but immediately afterwards descended again, briefly, to ankle-length. The new freedom of shorter skirts was not to be easily relinquished, however, and by about 1925 skirt lengths had settled to mid-knee or just below. Similarly, once women had discarded tight boned corsets they were unwilling to be imprisoned by them again. The characteristic silhouette of the Twenties was the opposite of the ultra-feminine Edwardian hourglass figure: the ideal was a slim, boyish look, denying natural curves. This, ironically, still required the wearing of constricting undergarments by those who were too well-endowed to be fashionable.

The natural waist disappeared and the 'waistline' descended to hip-level. Overblouses became popular, maintaining the low-waisted style. They were usually made of crêpe de Chine, but knitted silk and wool jersey were also much used. The 1920s Cable Sweater (see photograph, page 144) is faithful to this line: the vertical patterning emphasizing the long, slinky look is a typical Twenties feature. This design also reflects the increasing popularity of knitted clothes in the Twenties, when a separate wardrobe for sports and casual wear became *de rigueur,* and the cable-stitch bands recall tennis and cricket sweaters. But the openwork panels and decoration of shells and tiny pearl and crystal beads take this sweater far away from the sports field and transform it into a flattering evening style. Soft, pale, neutral colours, the peach and grey used here, and also beige, cream and brown (featured in the embroidered panels of the 1920s Art Deco Jacket, see photograph, page 137), were very popular and set off to perfection the jewel accessory of the Jazz Age – long ropes of pearls.

The sweater is knitted in a viscose yarn to suggest the sheen of real silk. Although 'artificial silk' (rayon) became widely available in the Twenties, top Paris designers shunned its use and still relied on the finest natural fibres, decorated with fur, feathers and intricately beaded embroidery, to assert their superiority now that the cut and line of clothes had become simpler and easier to imitate, and thereby less exclusive.

The post-war period saw a great revival in Paris fashion – the French textile industry was re-established with government aid and manufacturers vied with each other to produce rich and sumptuous fabrics for top couturiers such as Poiret, Lanvin, Paquin, Worth and Vionnet. Famous artists – Dufy is an outstanding example – produced imaginative designs for printed textiles, and an eclectic range of influences could be seen in couture fabrics, from Bakst's exotic designs for the Ballets Russes to African, Oriental and Egyptian sources, the latter becoming popular after the discovery of Tutankhamun's tomb in 1922.

All these influences were assimilated into the style that became known as Art Deco, which provides the inspiration for the stylized flower motif in the jacket panels. At first Art Deco took the characteristic curves and tendrils of Art Nouveau and formalized them into stricter, more geometric designs; flowers were a popular motif – the abstract angular designs usually associated with Art Deco were a later development.

The jacket is knitted in black angora – both yarn and colour were Twenties

Coat and skirt with matching hat by Paul Poiret, 1923, illustrated by A. E. Marty in Gazette du Bon Ton. *Skirts were still long at this date.*

favourites. Black was popular both as a background for printed designs and on its own; 'the little black dress' first became a staple of the chic wardrobe in the Twenties, and coats and jackets were often black or navy blue. Styles for coats were loose, waistless and often asymmetrical, fastening on the hip or shoulder. Fur was widely used for trimming as well as for complete coats, jackets and capes. Fluffy long-haired furs such as fox, and even monkey, were in vogue and this jacket recreates the fur look with bands of looped mohair for the cuffs, hemline and the detachable high collar.

The essential Twenties headgear was the cloche hat, and the angora jacket has its own matching version. A small neat head was a necessary element of the new narrow silhouette, and since elaborate hairstyles were obviously impossible under the close-fitting cloche, women 'bobbed' their hair – another blow for freedom which was considered shocking by many at the time. The cloche hat was worn low over the forehead, almost concealing the eyes; to emphasize the features, which would otherwise have lacked impact, even 'respectable' women started to wear make-up, which previously had been thought 'fast'. The emancipation of women – at least in fashion terms – had progressed further and faster than ever before!

1920s ART DECO JACKET

MEASUREMENTS (see also page 171)

Three sizes	small	medium	large
To fit bust:	81-86cm (32-34in)	91-96cm (36-38in)	102-107cm (40-42in)
Actual measurement:	98cm (38½in)	104cm (41in)	110cm (43½in)
Length from shoulder:	72.5cm (28½in)	74.5cm (29in)	77.5cm (30.5in)
Sleeve seam:	43cm (17in)	46cm (18in)	48cm (19in)

VERSION 1

MATERIALS
Yarn
Use double-knit weight: 525(550 : 575)g/19(20 :
21)oz black angora (A), 50g(2oz) cream cotton (B),
25g(1oz) grey viscose (C), 100g(4oz) brown viscose
(D), 75g(3oz) brown mohair (E)

Needles and other materials
1 pair each of 3¾mm (US 5), 4½mm
(US 7) and 5½mm (US 9) needles
5 buttons
9 press-studs
2 hook and eye fasteners

Tension
20 sts and 26 rows to 10cm (4in) on 4½mm
needles and st st using angora yarn.

RIGHT FRONT
**With 3¾mm needles and yarn A, cast on 69
(72 : 75) sts.
Row 1: (RS facing) K1(0 : 1), *P1, K1, rep from *
to end.

NOTE
● When working from chart, wind off small
amounts of the required colours so that
each motif can be worked separately. Twist
yarns around each other on wrong side at
joins to avoid holes.

Row 2: *P1, K1, rep from * to last 1(0 : 1) sts,
P1(0 : 1).
Rep the last 2 rows for 5cm (2in), ending with a
2nd row.**
Change to 4½mm needles. Starting with a K row,
cont working in st st from chart.
Cont until row 52 of chart has been worked.
Now cont in st st using A only until front
measures 46(48 : 51)cm/18(19 : 20)in from cast-on
edge, ending with a P row.

***Shape neck**
Row 1: K2 tog, K to end.
Row 2: P to last 2 sts, K tog.
Row 3: K.
Row 4: P to last 2 sts, K2 tog.

KEY

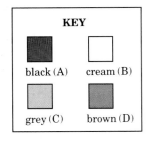

black (A)   cream (B)

grey (C)   brown (D)

opposite
*Version 1: black angora
1920s jacket trimmed with
two panels worked in an Art
Deco-style motif in grey,
cream and light brown. The
jacket has a mohair 'fur'
collar, which matches the
bottom and cuff edging, and
is fastened with large pearl
buttons; it is worn with a
matching cloche hat.*

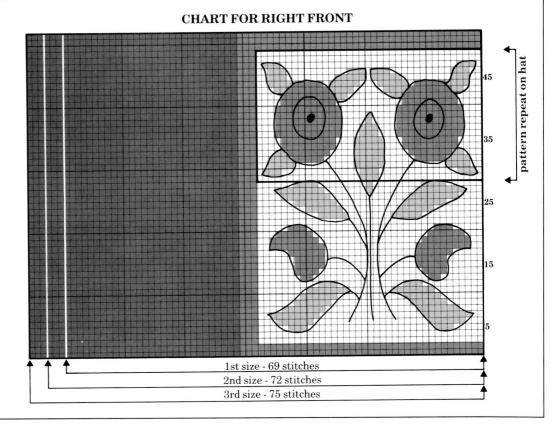

CHART FOR RIGHT FRONT

pattern repeat on hat

45
35
25
15
5

1st size - 69 stitches
2nd size - 72 stitches
3rd size - 75 stitches

Row 5: K2 tog, K to end.
Row 6: P.
Rep the last 6 rows until 30(33 : 36) sts rem.
Work 11 rows straight in st st.
Shape shoulder
Cast off 10(11 : 12) sts at beg of next and 2 foll
alt rows.

LEFT FRONT
Work as for right front from ** to **.
Change to 4½mm needles and starting with a K
row cont in st st until front measures 25 rows less
than right front to start of shoulder shaping
ending with a K row.

Shape neck
Cast off 30 sts at beg of next row – 39(42 : 45) sts.
Now work as for right front from *** to end,
reversing neck shaping.

BACK
With 3¾mm needles and A, cast on 98(104 : 110)
sts and work in K1, P1 rib for 5cm (2in).
Change to 4½mm needles and starting with a K
row cont in st st until back measures same as
front to start of shoulder shaping, ending with
a P row.

Shape shoulders
Cast off 10(11 : 12) sts at beg of next 6 rows – 38
sts. Cast off.

SLEEVES
With 3¾mm needles and A, cast on 48 sts and
work in K1, P1 rib for 5cm (2in).
Increase row: Rib and inc in every 2nd st across
row – 72 sts.
Change to 4½mm needles and starting with a K
row cont in st st, inc 1 st at each end of 3rd and
every foll 4th row until there are 94 sts.
Work straight until sleeve measures 43(46 :
48)cm/17(18 : 19)in from cast-on edge, ending
with a P row.
Cast off.

FLORAL COLLAR
With 4½mm needles and B, cast on 4 sts.
Starting with a K row, cont in st st working from
chart, working shaping as indicated until row 84
of chart has been worked.
Cast off.

POCKETS
Make 2. With 4½mm needles and A, cast on 3
sts. Starting with a K row, cont in st st inc 1 st at
beg of 3rd and every foll alt row until there are
22 sts.
Work straight in st st until pocket measures
28cm(11in) from cast-on edge, ending with a P
row. Dec 1st at beg of next and every foll alt row
until 3 sts rem. Cast off.

TO MAKE UP
Join shoulder seams. With centre of cast-off edge
of sleeves to shoulder seams, position sleeves,
reaching down to same depth on back and fronts.
Sew in position.
Join sleeve and side seams, leaving an opening
for pockets.
Press pockets, fold with RS together and join
shaped edges. Stitch into pocket openings.
With A, embroider floral collar and front panel.
Using a backstitch or chain stitch outline the
leaves, flowers and stems as indicated on chart
(Diagram 1). Sew floral collar to shaped edge of
right front **(Diagram 2)**.

Right front rib
With 3¾mm needles and D, with RS facing, pick
up and K 92(96 : 100) sts evenly up right front
edge to start of floral collar.
Work 4 rows K1, P1 rib. Cast off loosely in rib.

Floral collar rib
With 3¾mm needles and D, and with RS facing,
pick up and K 56 sts along lower edge of floral
collar. Work 4 rows K1, P1 rib.
Cast off in rib.
Sew in all ends, join edges of right front rib and
floral collar rib.
Stitch through edge of floral collar and right front
to hold in place **(Diagram 3)**.

Left front rib
With 3¾mm needles and A, with RS facing, pick
up and K120(124 : 128)sts evenly from left front
edge. Work 4 rows K1, P1 rib.
Cast off loosely in rib.

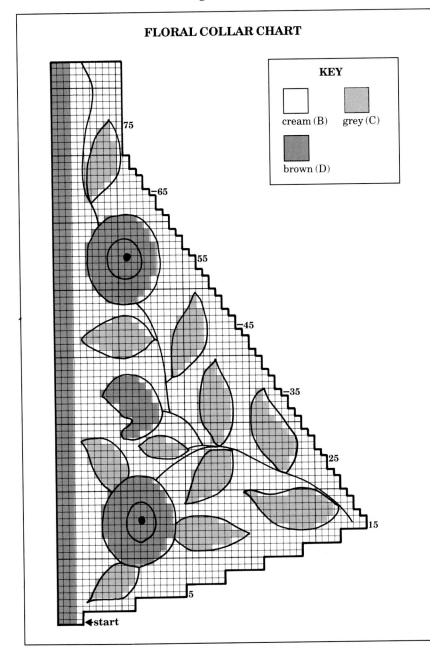

FLORAL COLLAR CHART

KEY

cream (B)   grey (C)

brown (D)

75

65

55

45

35

25

15

5

◄start

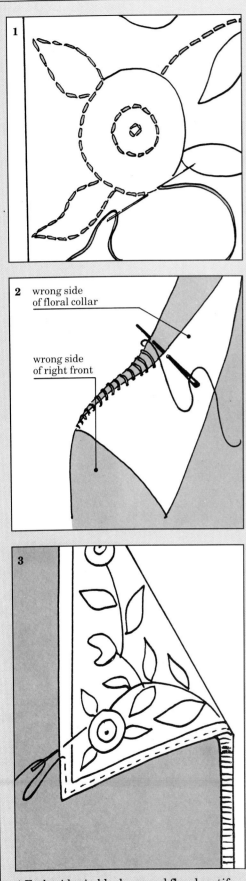

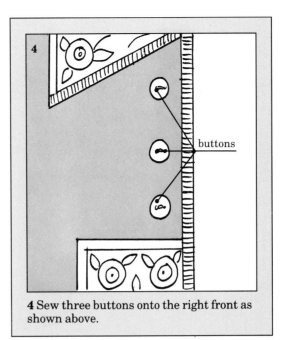

4 Sew three buttons onto the right front as shown above.

1 Embroider in black around floral motifs on front panel and floral collar. **2** Sew floral collar to shaped edge of right front . **3** Stitch edge of floral collar to right front to hold in place, using matching yarn.

Collar

With 3¾mm needles and A, with RS facing, pick up and K 32 sts across back neck and 44 sts from left front neck – 76 sts.
Change to 4½mm needles.
Next row: Cast on 10 sts, P to end – 86 sts.
Starting with a K row cont in st st until collar measures 3cm(1¼in) ending with a K row.
Next row: (buttonhole row) P5, cast off 3 sts, P to end.
Next row: K to end, casting on 3 sts over those cast off in previous row.
Work a further 3cm(1¼in) st st, ending with a K row then rep buttonhole rows.
Work 3cm(1¼in) st st.
Cast off loosely.
Sew 3 buttons to right front as shown **(Diagram 4)**.
Sew 2 buttons on collar.
Sew 3 press-studs behind buttons on fronts, place 3 evenly up front edge and sew 2 at neck edge of collar and 1 at beg of collar.

FUR COLLAR

With 5½mm needles and using D and E tog, cast on 10 sts.
Row 1: (WS facing) K.
Row 2: *K1 but do not sl st from needle, yf and over LH thumb to make a loop approx 2.5cm(1in), take yarn back and K same st again in ordinary way, yf and over RH needle, sl last 2 sts over loop, rep from * to end.
The last 2 rows form the patt. Rep the last 2 rows until collar measures 46cm(18in) from the cast-on edge.
Cast off.

TO MAKE UP

Sew 2 hook and eye fasteners to the short edges of fur collar.

FUR CUFFS

Make 2. With 5½mm needles and D and E tog, cast on 4 sts.
Cont in patt as for fur collar until cuff measures 23cm(9in) from cast-on edge.
Cast off.

LOWER EDGING

Work as for fur cuffs until edging is long enough to fit entire lower edge of jacket.
Cast off.

Stitch cuffs and lower edging in place on top of rib on garment.

VERSION 2

MATERIALS
Yarn
Use double-knit weight: 525(550 : 575)g/19(20 : 21)oz black cotton (A), 50g(2oz) yellow cotton (B), 25g(1oz) green cotton (C), 50g(2oz) pink cotton (D)
Needles and other materials
1 pair each 3¾mm (US 5) and 4½mm (US 7) needles
7 buttons
9 press-studs
Tension as Version 1.

METHOD
Work as for Version 1 but omit fur collar, cuffs and lower edging.
Sew 5 buttons to fronts, arranged to look as if double-breasted.

VERSION 3

MATERIALS
Yarn
Use double-knit weight: 375(400 : 425)g/14(15 : 15)oz black angora (A), 200(225 : 225)g/8oz cream cotton (B), 50g(2oz) pink cotton (D)
Needles and other materials
1 pair each 3¾mm (US 5) and 4½mm (US 7) needles
5 buttons
9 press-studs
Tension as Version 1.

METHOD
Work as for Version 1 but work floral panel of charts entirely in B.
Work left front and back in A but substitute B for A on sleeves.
Omit fur collar, cuffs and lower edging and embroidery.

CLOCHE HAT

MEASUREMENTS (see also page 171)
One size to fit an average head

VERSION 1

MATERIALS
Yarn
Use double-knit weight: 25g(1oz) each black angora (A), cream cotton (B), grey viscose (C), brown viscose (D)
Needles
1 pair each 3¾mm (US 5) and 4½mm (US 7) needles
Tension as Version 1 angora jacket

METHOD
With 3¾mm needles and D, cast on 111 sts.
Starting with a K row work 10 rows st st.
Change to 4½mm needles and yarn A. Work 4 rows st st. Now, starting with a K row cont in st st working from chart as indicated.
Work rows 29-49.
Cont in st st and A only. Work 2 rows.
Decrease row: *P1, P2 tog, rep from * to end – 74 sts.
Starting with a K row work 7 rows st st.
Decrease row: P2, *P2 tog, P1, rep from * to end – 50 sts.
Starting with a K row work 5 rows st st.
Decrease row: *P2 tog, rep from * to end – 25 sts. Starting with a K row work 3 rows st st.
Decrease row: P1, *P2 tog, rep from * to end – 13 sts.
Next row: K.
Decrease row: P1, *P2 tog, rep from * to end – 7 sts. Thread yarn through rem sts, draw up and fasten off securely.

TO MAKE UP
Sew in all ends and press following instructions on ball band. Join seam. Embroider outlines on floral motifs as for Version 1 angora jacket.

VERSION 2

CLOCHE HAT WITH PINK FLORAL MOTIF

MATERIALS
Yarn
Use double-knit weight: 25g(1oz) each black angora(A), cream cotton (B), grey viscose (C), pink cotton(D)
Needles and tension as Version 1.

METHOD
Work as for Version 1, but substituting pink cotton for brown viscose(D).

Version 2: this jacket is worked in cotton throughout. The colours on the floral motif change to bright pink and green on a yellow ground. Five buttons are used on the front to give a double-breasted look.

Version 3: the body of the jacket is knitted in black angora while the sleeves and panels are in cream cotton; the panels are left plain, but edged in bright pink. There is a matching hat (Version 2).

1920s CABLE SWEATER

MEASUREMENTS (see also page 172)

Three sizes	small	medium	large
To fit bust:	81-86cm (32-34in)	91-96cm (36-38in)	102-107cm (40-42in)
Actual measurement:	96cm (38in)	102cm (40in)	107cm (42in)
Length from shoulder:	64cm (25in)	66cm (26in)	69cm (27in)
Sleeve seam:	47cm (18½in)	47cm (18½in)	47cm (18½in)

VERSION 1

MATERIALS
Yarn
Use double-knit weight: 575(600 : 625)g/21(22 : 22)oz cream viscose (A), 150g(6oz) grey viscose/cotton mix (B)

Needles and other materials
1 pair each of 3¼mm (US 4) and 4mm (US 6) needles
Cable needle
28 sew-on shells
300 small pearl beads
200 small crystal beads

Tension
22 sts and 27 rows to 10cm (4in) on 4mm needles and st st using viscose yarn.

> **NOTE**
> • Any double-knit weight yarn can be used, as long as the tension is the same as that given above.

BACK
With 3¼mm needles and A, cast on 108(114 : 120) sts.
Row 1: (RS facing) K0(2 : 0), *P2, K2, rep from * to end.
Row 2: *P2, K2, rep from * to last 0(2 : 0) sts, P0(2 : 0).
Rep last the 2 rows for 5cm (2in), ending with a 2nd row. Change to 4mm needles and work in patt as follows:
Row 1: (RS facing) K5(8 : 11), *P2, K8, P2, K8, P2, K16, rep from * once more, P2, K8, P2, K8, P2, K5(8 : 11).
Row 2: P5(8 : 11), *K1, pick up and K the bar that lies between st just worked and next st on LH needle – called M1, K1, P8, K1, M1, K1, P8, K1, M1, K1, P16, rep from * once more, K1, M1, K1, P8, K1, M1, K1, P8, K1, M1, K1, P5(8 : 11) –117(123 : 129) sts.
Row 3: K5(8 : 11), *P3, K8, P3, K8, P3, K16, rep from * once more, P3, K8, P3, K8, P3, K5(8 : 11).
Row 4: P5(8 : 11), *K3, P8, K3, P8, K3, P16, rep from * once more, K3, P8, K3, P8, K3, P5(8 : 11).
Rows 5-6: Rep rows 3-4.
Row 7: K5(8 : 11), *P3, sl next 4 sts onto cable needle and hold at back of work, K4, then K4 from cable needle* rep from * to * once more, P3, K16, rep from * to * twice more, P3, K16, rep from * to * twice more, P3, K5(8 : 11).
Row 8: As row 4.
Rows 9-10: Rep rows 3-4.

Rows 3-10 form the patt.
Cont in patt until back measures 64(66 : 69)cm/25(26 : 27)in from cast-on edge, ending with a WS row.
Next row: K5(8 : 11), *P1, allow next st to drop off needle – called drop 1, P1, K8, P1, drop 1, P1, K8, P1, drop 1, P1, K16, rep from * once more, P1, drop 1, P1, K8, P1, drop 1, P1, K8, P1, drop 1, P1, K5(8 : 11) – 108(114 : 120) sts.

Shape shoulders
Cast off 9(10 : 11) sts at beg of next 6 rows – 54 sts.
Cast off.

FRONT
Work as for back until front measures 48(50 : 53)cm/19(20 : 21)in from cast-on edge, ending with a RS row.

Shape neck
Next row: Patt 46(49 : 52) sts, *K1, drop 1, K1, P8, * rep from * to * once more, K1, drop 1, K1, patt to end – 114(120 : 126) sts.
Next row: Patt 46(49 : 52), cast off centre 22 sts, patt to end and cont on this last set of sts only.
**Dec 1 st at neck edge on every row until 30(33 : 36) sts rem.
Cont straight until front measures the same as back to start of shoulder shaping, ending with a WS row.**
Next row: *P1, drop 1, P1, K8, rep from * ending last rep K5(8 : 11) – 27(30 : 33) sts.

Shape shoulder
Cast off 9(10 : 11) sts at beg of next and 2 foll alt rows.
With WS facing rejoin yarn to rem sts and work as for first side from **to **.
Next row: K5(8 : 11), P1, drop 1, P1, *K8, P1, drop 1, P1, rep from * to end – 27(30 : 33) sts.

Shape shoulder
Cast off 9(10 : 11) sts at beg of 3 foll alt rows.

SLEEVES
Make 2. With 3¼mm needles and A, cast on 48 sts and work in K2, P2 rib for 5cm (2in).
Increase row: Rib and inc 1 st in every 2nd st across row – 72 sts.
Change to 4mm needles. Starting with a K row, cont in st st and stripe sequence of 16 rows B, 16 rows A, at the same time, inc 1 st at each end of 3rd and every foll 4th row until there are 110 sts on the needle.
Work straight until 112 rows have been worked in stripe sequence.
Cast off.

TO MAKE UP

Allow the dropped sts to unravel down the work, forming ladders. Press pieces carefully following ball band instructions. Join left shoulder seam.

Neckband

With 3¼mm needles and A, and with RS facing, pick up and K 54 sts across back neck, 36 sts down left side of neck, 22 sts from centre front neck and 36 sts up right side of neck – 148 sts. Work in K2, P2 rib for 2.5cm(1in). Cast off in rib.

Join right shoulder and neckband seam. With centre of cast-off edges of sleeves to shoulder seams, position sleeves, reaching down to same depth on back and front. Sew in position. Join side and sleeve seams, matching stripes. Sew the shells at even intervals between cables. Place 8 on the centre panel and 10 on each side panel (**Diagram 1**).
Sew one pearl bead and one crystal bead alternately on sleeves, along the first row of every stripe (**Diagram 2**). Sew pearl beads at inner neck edge round front neckband.

VERSION 2

BLACK VISCOSE SWEATER WITH PINK STRIPED SLEEVES

This version is worked as for Version 1 substituting black viscose for cream viscose (A) and pink cotton for grey viscose/cotton (B). Omit all bead and shell decoration.

VERSION 3

SWEATER IN ONE COLOUR ONLY

MATERIALS
Yarn
Use double-knit weight: 725(750 : 775)g/26(27 : 28)oz cotton/viscose mix in chosen colour
Needles and tension as Version 1.

METHOD
Work as for Version 1 but using one colour throughout and omit all decoration.

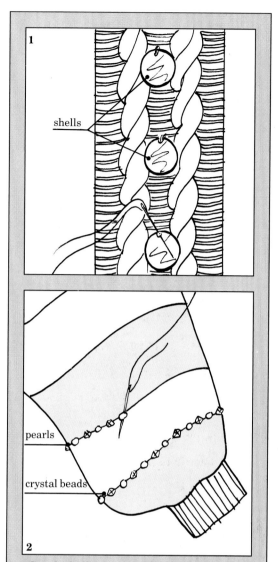

shells

pearls

crystal beads

1 Stitch shells at even intervals between the cables. **2** Alternate pearls and crystal beads along the first row of every stripe on the sleeves.

opposite
Version 1: slinky cable sweater knitted in pinky-beige viscose with grey-striped sleeves. The front of the sweater is decorated with three bands of shells and the sleeves are trimmed with pearls and crystal beads.

Version 2: eye-catching version of the cable sweater knitted in black viscose with shocking pink striped sleeves.

Version 3: the sweater looks sophisticated knitted in a pale grey cotton/viscose mixture.

THE THIRTIES AND FORTIES
INTRODUCTION

The characteristic silhouette of women's clothes in the Thirties did not at first differ greatly from the long, lean, waistless outline of the Twenties. Later in the decade, though, there was a movement towards more curvaceous lines. The waist was more clearly defined and the shoulders became broader – a look that was to develop into the very square padded shoulders and nipped-in waist of the war years and after.

The gradual rejection of the straight up-and-down line and the adoption of a more flattering feminine shape was partly due to

Fashions worn in Paris during the Second World War display characteristic features of the period: square, padded shoulders, fitted waists, a loose fur-trimmed jacket and turban-style hats.

the influence of Hollywood films. With the collapse of the American stock market and the mass unemployment of the Depression years, there was a yearning for the glamorous escapism of Hollywood. Fashion was naturally influenced by women's desire to copy the looks of their favourite stars – sultry screen goddesses such as Garbo and Joan Crawford. Slinky bias-cut evening gowns in satin and silk crêpe as worn by Jean Harlow became Thirties classics; fur trims on jackets and coats added the requisite touch of glamour for day and evening. The fluffy mohair shawl collar of the Raglan Jacket (see photograph, page 151) gives the same softly flattering neckline as the favourite fox fur or marabou feathers of the period.

The style of the jacket also owes something to Coco Chanel (1883-1971), whose career as a major designer spanned half a century. She was perhaps the first couturier to introduce wealthy customers to the concept of understated 'throwaway' elegance. Casual cardigan jackets with turned back cuffs and revers, or collarless fronts meeting edge to edge, were worn with a white shirt and masses of fake gold chains or pearls (Chanel was also the originator of costume jewellery). This is one of the few twentieth-century styles to have remained fashionable for over thirty years.

Sue Bradley's choice of colours for the jacket are in keeping with the subtle, sludgy pastels favoured in the Thirties: eau-de-Nil, duck-egg blue, cream and dusky shades of pink, grey and yellow were much used, as well as ever-chic black, white and navy blue. The pattern – irregular geometric shapes combined with an abstract floral motif – is typical of the Art Deco style which dominated not only textiles but all the decorative arts in this period. Inspiration for this design comes from the pottery of Clarice Cliff (1900-1970), one of the most inventive and original English ceramic designers of the Twenties and Thirties. Her tableware, particularly the 'Bizarre' and 'Fantasque' ranges which are now collectors' items, featured brightly coloured abstract designs.

A broad, ribbed turban in dusky pink mohair matches one of the shades of the jacket. It echoes the turban look fashionable in the Thirties, when it would have been worn with softly curled shoulder-length or pageboy-styled hair.

As a contrast to the high fashion jacket, the other design in this section is a V-necked Fair Isle Sweater (see photograph, page 159), as wearable now as in the Twenties and Thirties – the period when it graduated from being an ethnic working garment knitted by Fair Islanders for their own use to an international classic for sports and casual wear.

Fair Isle knitting is a method of patterned knitting, traditionally using two colours in each row, with the wool not in use being looped along the back of the work. The double thickness makes garments knitted in this way extra warm and waterproof.

Fair Isle itself is one of the Shetland isles off the north-east coast of Scotland – islands where hand-knitting has been a major cottage industry since the sixteenth century. In the early 1900s the Fair Isle style of knitting became common throughout the Shetlands, where it is still a flourishing skill today.

The craft of knitting probably began in the islands because of the availability of excellent wool from the native sheep. The derivation of the characteristic patterns is more of a mystery, but the traditional local explanation is that a sailor brought home from abroad a patterned shawl which the Fair Islanders copied. The provenance of this possibly mythical object may have been the Baltic states, where there was a long tradition of patterned stranded knitting.

What does seem certain is that Fair Isle designs as we know them were first developed around 1850, a date which corresponds with the first known use of imported dyes. Early Shetland knitting used colour combinations derived solely from

Portrait of HRH The Prince of Wales (later Edward VIII) painted in 1925 by John St Helier Lander. The Prince is shown wearing a Fair Isle sweater.

natural wool shades from differently coloured fleeces: white, cream, fawn, grey and dark brown. Fair Isle knitters also used natural dyes obtained from local plants and lichens growing on the rocks to obtain soft rose, pale gold and purple-brown shades, but it was the arrival of imported madder – giving rich red and indigo (deep blue) – which first enabled the familiar colourful designs to evolve.

The rage for Fair Isle patterned knitwear was given its first impetus in 1921, when a firm of drapers at Lerwick in the Shetlands presented a Fair Isle sweater to the then Prince of Wales (Edward VIII) on the occasion of his visit to Scotland to play golf at St Andrew's. Local knitters gladly responded to the new enthusiasm for their products and began to turn out more and more all-over patterned jerseys rather than applying the Fair Isle patterns to smaller items such as caps, scarves and socks, which had previously been the custom. The scale of production increased greatly with the availability of machine-spun, commercially dyed yarn of consistent quality.

Sue Bradley uses double-knitting yarn in traditional misty heathery Shetland colours to give an intricate but soft all-over effect for the Fair Isle Sweater. Add shoulder pads to give the current fashionable square-shouldered look – which is also how it would have been worn in the Thirties and Forties. The matching ribbed skirt is knitted straight and long in one of the greys of the sweater. Its straight tube shape is very much of the Thirties and Forties, a style in vogue at the moment.

RAGLAN JACKET

MEASUREMENTS (see also page 172)

Two sizes	small-medium	medium-large
To fit bust:	81-91cm (32-36in)	91-102cm (36-40in)
Actual measurement:	105cm (41½in)	114cm (45in)
Length from shoulder:	76cm (30in)	78cm (30¾in)
Sleeve seam:	33cm (13in)	33cm (13in)

VERSION 1

MATERIALS
Yarn
Use mohair, chunky and double-knit weight.
500(525)g/18(19)oz blue DK wool worked double
(A), 175(200)g/7(8)oz blue mohair (B), 225(250)g/
8(9)oz mohair/cotton mix (C), 100g(4oz) yellow
mohair (D), 75g(3oz) pink mohair (E), 50g(2oz)
brown mohair (F), 25g(1oz) green wool (G), 50g
(2oz) white mohair (H)
Needles and other materials
1 pair each of 4mm (US 6), 5mm
(US 8) and 6mm (US 10) needles
8 buttons
2 stitch holders

Tension
15 sts and 19 rows to 10cm (4in) on 6mm needles
and st st using mohair yarn.

> **NOTE**
> ● Use separate balls of yarn for each colour
> area worked, twisting yarns around each
> other on wrong side at joins to avoid holes.

BACK
With 5mm needles and A double, cast on 78
(84) sts.
Row 1: K2(0), *P2, K2, rep from * to end.
Row 2: *P2, K2, rep from * to last 2(0) sts, P2(0).
Rep the last 2 rows for 5cm (2in), ending with a
2nd row.
Change to 6mm needles.
Starting with a K row, cont working in st st from
chart (see page 152 for back and fronts chart).
Cont until row 74 of chart has been worked.

Shape raglan armholes
Work decs for raglan shaping as indicated until
row 134(138) has been worked. Cast off rem
18(20) sts.

RIGHT FRONT
With 5mm needles and A double cast on 67
(70) sts.
Row 1: (RS facing) P1(2), *K2, P2, rep from
* to end.
Row 2: *K2, P2, rep from * to last 1(2) sts, K1(2).
Rep the last 2 rows twice more.
Next row: (buttonhole row) Rib 6, cast off 3 sts,
rib 18, cast off 3 sts, rib to end.
Next row: Rib to end, casting on 3 sts over those
cast off in previous row.
Cont in rib until front measures 5cm (2in) from
cast-on edge, ending with a 1st row.

Next row: Rib 31 (34) sts and turn leaving rem
36 sts on a stitch holder.
**Change to 6mm needles.
Starting with a K row, cont working in st st from
chart where indicated.
Cont until row 74 of chart has been worked.

Shape raglan armhole
Work decs for raglan shaping as indicated until
row 134 (138) has been worked.
Cast off rem 1 (2) sts.

LEFT FRONT
With 5mm needles and A double cast on 67
(70) sts.
Row 1: (RS facing) *P2, K2, rep from * to last 1
(2) sts, P1(2).
Row 2: K1(2), *P2, K2, rep from * to end.
Rep the last 2 rows for 5cm (2in), ending with a
1st row.
Next row: Rib 36 sts and sl onto a stitch holder,
rib to end – 31 (34) sts.
Work as for right front from ** to end, reading
chart where indicated and reversing shaping.

SLEEVES
Make 2. With 5mm needles and A double, cast on
48 (54) sts.
Row 1: (RS facing) K0(2), *P2, K2, rep from
* to end.
Row 2: *P2, K2, rep from * to last 0(2) sts, P0(2).
Rep the last 2 rows for 5cm (2in), ending with a
2nd row.
Change to 6mm needles.
Starting with a K row, cont working in st st from
chart (see page 153) inc 1 st at each end of 3rd
row and 20 foll alt rows – 90(96) sts.
Cont straight until row 54 of the chart has
been worked.

Shape raglan top
Work decs for raglan shaping as indicated until
row 114(118) has been worked.
Cast off rem 10 sts.

TO MAKE UP
Sew in all ends and lightly steam the work on
wrong side.

Raglan ribs
Make 4. With 5mm needles and A double and RS
facing, pick up and K 52(56) sts evenly along
raglan edges of sleeve top.
Work in K2, P2 rib for 8 rows.
Cast off in rib (**Diagram 1** see page 154).

Pockets
Make 2. With 4mm needles and yarn A used
single cast on 3 sts.
Starting with a K row, cont in st st inc 1 st at beg
of 3rd and every foll alt row until there are 26 sts.
Work straight until pocket measures 25cm (10in)
from cast-on edge, ending with a P row.
Dec 1 st at beg of next and every foll alt row until
3 sts rem ending with a P row.
Cast off.
Press pockets, fold RS tog and join shaped edges.
Set in raglan sleeves.

BACK AND FRONTS CHART

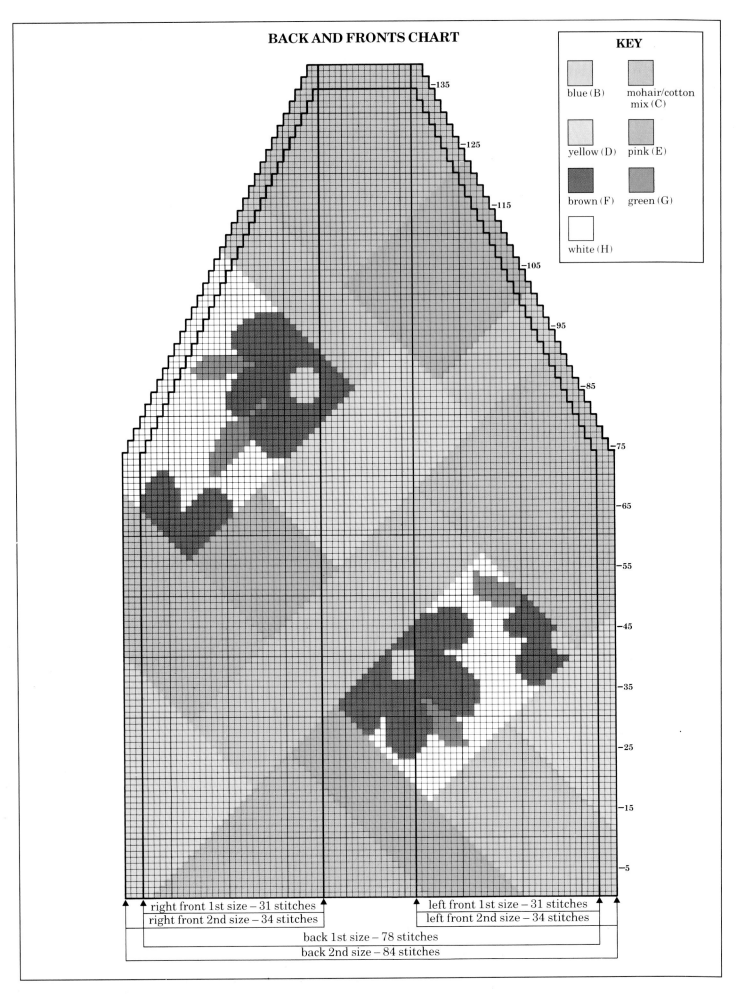

KEY

blue (B)   mohair/cotton mix (C)

yellow (D)   pink (E)

brown (F)   green (G)

white (H)

−135
−125
−115
−105
−95
−85
−75
−65
−55
−45
−35
−25
−15
−5

right front 1st size − 31 stitches
right front 2nd size − 34 stitches

left front 1st size − 31 stitches
left front 2nd size − 34 stitches

back 1st size − 78 stitches
back 2nd size − 84 stitches

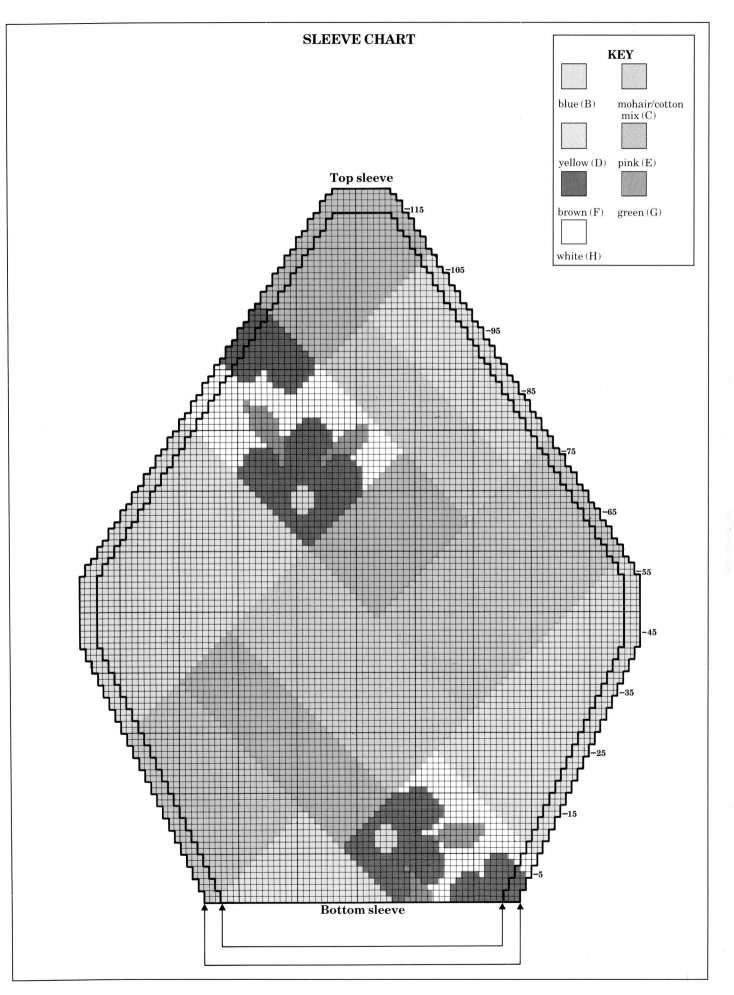

SLEEVE CHART

KEY

blue (B)   mohair/cotton
                  mix (C)

yellow (D)   pink (E)

brown (F)   green (G)

white (H)

Top sleeve

—115

—105

—95

—85

—75

—65

—55

—45

—35

—25

—15

—5

Bottom sleeve

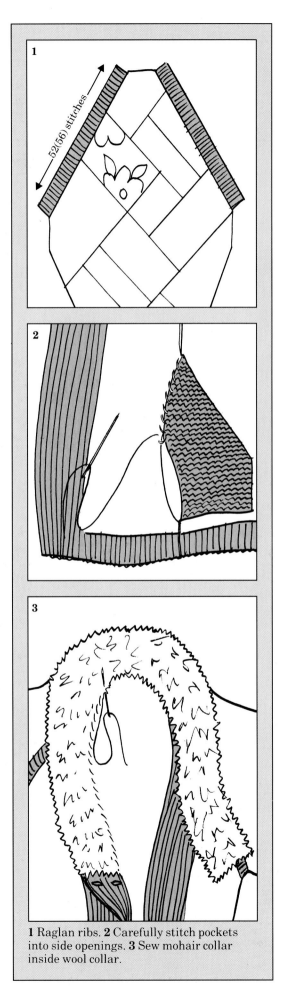

Join sleeve seams.
Mark the position of pockets on side seams, to start approx 15cm (6in) above cast-on edge.
Join remainder of side seams.
Carefully stitch pockets into side openings (**Diagram 2**).

Button band
With 5mm needles, A double and RS facing, rejoin yarn to sts on stitch holder of left front.
Cont in rib as set until band, when slightly stretched, fits up front edge and across to centre back neck.
Cast off in rib.

Buttonhole band
With 5mm needles, A double and WS facing, rejoin yarn to sts on stitch holder of right front.
Cont in rib as set making 3 further sets of buttonholes at 8.5cm(3½in) intervals from previous buttonholes.
Work in rib until buttonhole band is same length as button band.
Cast off in rib or leave sts on a length of yarn.
Sew bands to front edges and sew at centre back neck.
Sew on buttons.

Fluffy mohair collar
With 6mm needles and B double, cast on 20 sts.
Starting with a K row, cont in st st until collar fits from above last set of buttonholes on right front to a corresponding depth on left front.
Cast off loosely.
Sew collar, with K side as RS, inside wool collar of garment using a matching yarn (**Diagram 3**).
Brush up pile with a teasel or plastic brush.

See page 157 for Versions 2 and 3.

1 Raglan ribs. **2** Carefully stitch pockets into side openings. **3** Sew mohair collar inside wool collar.

Version 2: the same pattern given a jazzy treatment with bright colours including fuchsia, purple and turquoise.
The jacket has a plain ribbed collar and is worn with a matching turban.

Version 3: this is exactly the same as Version 1 but the colours change to subtle shades of brown, blue and green with black. Again it is worn with a turban.

VERSION 2

BRIGHT FLOWER JACKET WITHOUT FLUFFY COLLAR

MATERIALS
Yarn
Use mohair, chunky and double-knit weight. 500(525)g/18(19)oz purple DK wool worked double (A), 100(125)g/4(5)oz turquoise mohair (B), 225(250)g/8(9)oz mohair/cotton mix (C), 100g(4)oz yellow mohair (D), 75g(3)oz fuchsia mohair (E), 50g(2)oz navy mohair (F), 50g(2oz) lilac mohair (H)
Needles and other materials and tension as for Version 1.

METHOD
Work as for Version 1, but work yarn A for G. Omit fluffy collar.

VERSION 3

DARK FLOWER JACKET

MATERIALS
Yarn
Use mohair, chunky and double-knit weight. 500(525)g/18(19)oz black DK wool worked double (A), 175(200)g/7(8)oz black mohair (B), 225(250)g/8(9)oz mohair/cotton mix (C), 100g(4)oz dark brown mohair (D), 75g(3)oz deep blue mohair (E), 50g(2)oz bottle green mohair (F), 25g(1)oz olive green wool (G), 50g(2)oz dusky pink mohair (H)
Needles and other materials and tension as for Version 1.

METHOD
Work as for Version 1.

TURBAN

MEASUREMENTS
Approx width: 18cm (7in)

MATERIALS
Yarn
Use mohair weight: 45g(2oz) pink mohair
Needles
1 pair of 6mm (US 10) needles

Tension
20 sts and 20 rows to 10cm (4in) on 6mm needles and rib.

METHOD
With 6mm needles, cast on 36 sts work in K2, P2 rib until turban is long enough, when slightly stretched, to fit round head. Cast off loosely in rib.

TO MAKE UP
Join short ends of turban, then gather together along seam. Wrap a length of yarn over seam a few times to secure.

RIBBED SKIRT

MEASUREMENTS (see also page 172)

Three sizes	small	medium	large
To fit hips:	81-86cm (32-34in)	91-96cm (36-38in)	102-107cm (40-42in)
Actual measurement unstretched:	75cm (29½in)	86cm (34in)	96cm (38in)
Length:	91cm (36in)	91cm (36in)	91cm (36in)

MATERIALS
Yarn
Use double-knit weight: 400(450 : 500)g/15(16 : 18)oz grey wool
Needles and other materials
1 each of 3¼mm (US 4) and 4mm (US 6) circular needles. Waist length of 2.5cm(1in) wide elastic

Tension
26½ sts and 32 rows to 10cm(4in) on 4mm needles and moss rib unstretched.

METHOD
Beg at hem, with 4mm needle cast on 200(228 : 256) sts and work in moss rib as follows:
Round 1: *K3, P1, rep from * to end.

Round 2: P1, *K1, P3, rep from * to last 3 sts, K1, P2.
These rounds form the patt.
Cont in patt until skirt measures 91cm(36in) from beg.
Change to 3¼mm needle and work in rounds of K1, P1 rib for 8cm(3in).
With 4mm needle cast off loosely in rib.

TO MAKE UP
Fold ribbing in half onto wrong side and slip stitch down, leaving an opening to insert elastic. Thread elastic through waistband, secure ends and close opening.

See photograph on page 159.

FAIR ISLE SWEATER

VERSION 1 CHART

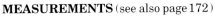

12-stitch
pattern
repeat

sleeves

back/front

KEY

pale blue (A)	blue (B)
brown (C)	pink (D)
white (E)	yellow (F)
grey (G)	turquoise (H)

opposite
Version 1: a fashion classic –
Fair Isle sweater knitted
in misty shades of blue,
brown, pink, yellow, grey
and turquoise with white.
The sweater has a deep V-
neck and ribbed welt and
cuffs; it is worn with a
matching ribbed tube skirt.

MEASUREMENTS (see also page 172)

Three sizes	small	medium	large
To fit bust:	81-86cm (32-34in)	91-96cm (36-38in)	102-107cm (40-42in)
Actual measurement:	90cm (35½in)	99cm (39in)	108cm (42½in)
Length from shoulder:	66cm (26in)	69cm (27in)	71cm (28in)
Sleeve seam:	43cm (17in)	46cm (18in)	48cm (19in)

VERSION 1

MATERIALS

Yarn
Use double-knit weight: 225(250 : 275)g/8(9 : 10)oz pale blue (A), 75(75 : 100)g/3(3 : 4)oz blue (B), 50(75 : 75)g/2(3 : 3)oz brown (C), 75(75 : 100)g/3(3 : 4)oz each pink (D), white (E), 50(75 : 75)g/2(3 : 3)oz each yellow (F), grey (G), 75(100 : 100)g/3(4 : 4)oz turquoise (H)

Needles
1 pair each of 3¼mm (US 4) and 4mm (US 6) needles

Tension
27 sts and 24 rows to 10cm (4in) on 4mm needles and Fair Isle patt.

NOTES

- Any double-knit weight yarn can be used, whether cotton or wool, as long as the tension is the same as that given above.

- When working Fair Isle patt, carry the yarn not in use loosely over the wrong side of the work over not more than 3 sts at a time to keep fabric elastic.

BACK
With 3¼mm needles and A, cast on 98(110 : 122) sts and work in double rib as follows:
Row 1: (RS facing) K2, *P2, K2, rep from * to end.
Row 2: P2, *K2, P2, rep from * to end.
Rep last 2 rows until rib measures 13cm (5in) ending with a 2nd row.
Increase row: Rib and inc 24 sts evenly across row – 122(134 : 146) sts.
Change to 4mm needles.
Next row: P.
Now work from chart, starting with a K row, work straight in st st until back measures 66(69 : 71)cm/26(27 : 28)in from cast-on edge, ending with a P row.

Shape shoulders
Cast off 10(11 : 12) sts at beg of next 6 rows and 9(10 : 11) sts at beg of foll 2 rows.
Leave rem 44(48 : 52) sts on a spare needle.

FRONT
Work as for back until front measures 38(41 : 43)cm/15(16 : 17)in from cast-on edge, ending with a P row.

Shape front neck
Next row: Patt 60(66 : 72) sts and turn, leaving rem sts on a spare needle. Cont on this set of sts only. **Keeping chart patt correct, dec 1 st at neck edge on 2nd and every foll 3rd (2nd : 2nd) row until 39(43 : 47) sts rem. Now work straight until front measures the same as back to start of shoulder shaping, ending at side edge.

Shape shoulder
Cast off 10(11 : 12) sts at beg of next row and 2 foll alt rows, then cast off 9(10 : 11) sts at beg of next alt row.
With RS facing, sl centre 2 sts onto a safety pin, rejoin yarn to rem sts, patt to end.
Work as for first side from ** to end.

SLEEVES
Make 2. With 3¼mm needles and A, cast on 48 sts and work in K2, P2 rib for 8cm (3in).
Increase row: Rib and inc 1 st in every st across row – 96 sts. Change to 4mm needles.
Next row: P.
Now work from chart, starting with a K row at row 17, cont in patt inc 1 st at each end of 2nd and every foll 3rd row until there are 132 sts.
Cont straight until sleeve measures 43(46 : 48)cm/17(18 : 19)in from cast-on edge, ending with a P row. Cast off.

TO MAKE UP
Sew in all ends and press lightly on WS following ball band instructions.
Join right shoulder seam.

Neckband
With 3¼mm needles and A and RS facing, pick up and K 72 sts down left side of neck, 2 sts from safety pin, 72 sts up right side of neck and K 44(48 : 52) sts across back neck – 190(194 : 198) sts.
Row 1: Work in K2, P2 rib to within 2 sts of centre front sts, P2 tog, K2, P2 tog tbl, work in K2, P2 rib to end.
Row 2: Rib to within 2 sts of centre front sts, K2 tog, P2, K2 tog tbl, rib to end.
Rep last 2 rows twice more, then 1st row again.
Cast off loosely in rib, dec on this row as before.
Join left shoulder and neckband working a chain st over centre front sts to form mock rib. With centre of cast-off edges of sleeves to shoulder seams, position sleeves, reaching down to same depth on back and front.
Sew in position. Join side and sleeve seams.

VERSION 2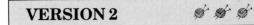

FAIR ISLE SWEATER WITH CREW NECK

MATERIALS
Yarn
Use double-knit weight: 225(250 : 275)g/8(9 : 10)oz dark purple (A), 75(75 : 100)g/3(3 : 4)oz lilac (B), 50(75 : 75)g/2(3 : 3)oz turquoise (C), 75(75 : 100)g/3(3 : 4)oz each yellow (D), fuchsia (E), 50 (75 : 75)g/2(3 :3)oz each light grey (F), dark grey (G), 75(100 : 100)g/3(4 : 4)oz dark blue (H)
Needles and tension as for Version 1.

BACK
Work as Version 1 following chart for Version 2.

FRONT
Work as for back until front measures 58(61 : 63)cm/23(24 : 25)in from cast-on edge, ending with a P row.

Shape front neck
Next row: Patt 49(55 : 61), turn and leave rem sts on a spare needle.
Cont on this set of sts only. **Dec 1 st at neck edge on every row until 39(43 :47) sts rem. Cont straight in patt until front measures the same as back to start of shoulder shaping, ending at the side edge.

Shape shoulder
Cast off 10(11 :12) sts at beg of next row and 2 foll alt rows, then cast off 9(10 :11) sts at beg of next alt row.
With RS facing, sl centre 24 sts onto a spare needle, rejoin yarn to rem sts, patt to end.
Work as for first side from ** to end.

SLEEVES AND TO MAKE UP
Work as for Version 1 following chart for Version 2.

Neckband
With 3¼mm needles and A, and RS facing, pick up and K 24 sts down left side of neck, K across 24 sts from spare needle at centre front, pick up and K 24 sts up right side of neck and then K across 44(48 : 52) sts at back neck – 116(120 : 124) sts.
Work in K2, P2 rib for 2.5cm(1in).
Cast off loosely in rib.

VERSION 3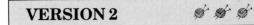

FAIR ISLE V-NECK SLIPOVER

MATERIALS
Yarn
Use double-knit weight: 150(175 : 200)g/6(7 : 8)oz black (A), 50g(2oz) white (B), 25(50 : 50)g/1(2 : 2)oz pale grey (C), 50g(2oz) light brown (D), dark blue (E), 25(50 : 50)g/1(2 :2)oz blue green (F), 50g(2oz) each dark brown (G), dark grey (H)
Needles and tension as for Version 1.

METHOD
Work back, front and neckband as for Version 1 following chart for Version 3. Join left shoulder and neckband. Mark depth of armholes 26cm (10in) down from shoulder on back and front.

Armhole edgings
With 3¼mm needles and A, and RS facing, pick up and K 120 sts evenly around armhole between markers. Work in K2, P2 rib for 2.5cm(1in).
Cast off in rib.
Join side seams.

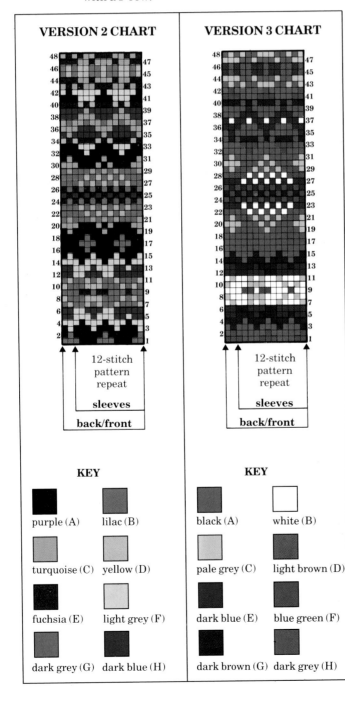

VERSION 2 CHART — **VERSION 3 CHART**

12-stitch pattern repeat

sleeves

back/front

KEY

purple (A) — lilac (B)
turquoise (C) — yellow (D)
fuchsia (E) — light grey (F)
dark grey (G) — dark blue (H)

KEY

black (A) — white (B)
pale grey (C) — light brown (D)
dark blue (E) — blue green (F)
dark brown (G) — dark grey (H)

Version 2: the same attractive Fair Isle pattern is given a different look by the use of bright colours including fuchsia, yellow and turquoise. This version has a round neck.

Version 3: a sleeveless V-necked style knitted in earthy shades including brown, blue-green and grey.

Decoration
Decorate the vertical stripes of red on front and back and horizontal red stripes on sleeves with the gold metal studs placed at 2.5cm(1in) intervals **(Diagram 1)**.
Decorate ribs on yoke, welt and cuffs with rhinestones **(Diagram 2)**.

VERSION 2

SWEATER STRIPED IN GREEN, BLUE AND BLACK WITH NO DECORATION

MATERIALS
Yarn
Use Aran wool and mohair: 225(250 : 275)g/ 8(9 : 10)oz black Aran wool (A), 100(125 : 150)g/ 4(5 : 6)oz blue mohair (B), 100(125 : 150)g/ 4(5 : 6)oz green mohair (C), 50(50 : 75)g/2(2 : 3)oz gold lurex - use 3 strands together (E)
This version is worked exactly as Version 1. The needles and tension are the same but omit the red stripes and work black instead, so substituting yarn A for yarn D throughout. All decoration is omitted.

VERSION 3

WORKED IN TWO COLOURS ONLY

MATERIALS
Yarn
Use Aran wool and mohair: 175(200 : 225)g/ 7(8 : 8)oz black Aran wool (A), 300(350 : 400)g/ 11(13 : 15)oz blue mohair (B)
Follow the pattern for Version 1, but substitute yarn A for E and substitute yarn B for yarns B, C and D.
Omit all decoration.

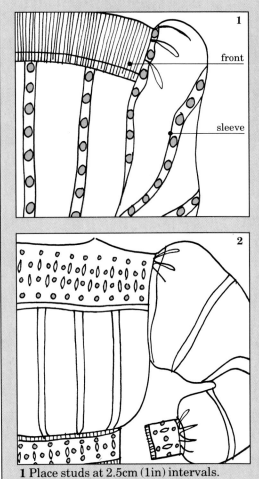

1 Place studs at 2.5cm (1in) intervals.
2 Decorate yoke, welt and cuffs.

VERSION 2

BLUE MOHAIR AND BLACK ARAN WAISTCOAT WITH PLAIN BLACK RIBS

MATERIALS
Yarns
100(125 : 150)g/4 (5 : 6)oz black Aran (A), 100 (100 : 125)g/4 (4 : 5)oz blue mohair (B)
Needles and tension as for Version 1.

METHOD
Back and fronts are worked as for Version 1, but substitute blue for pink. Make up as for Version 1.

Armhole edgings
Alike. With 4½mm needles and A and with RS facing, pick up and K 80 sts around one armhole edge. Work in K1, P1 rib for 2.5cm (1in) in A. Cast off in rib.
Join side seams and armhole edgings.

Bottom edging
With 4½mm needles and A and with RS facing, pick up and K 38(40 : 42)sts along bottom edge of front, 90(92 : 94)sts at back and 38(40 : 42)sts along other front edge – 166(172 : 178)sts.
Work in K1, P1 rib for 2.5cm (1in) in A.
Cast off in rib.

Front bands
Alike. With 4½mm needles and A, and RS facing, pick up and K 60 sts evenly along one front edge (including edge of bottom edging). Work in K1, P1 rib for 2.5cm (1in) in A. Cast off in rib.

Neck edging
Work as for neck edging on Version 1 but in A only and K1, P1 rib as for rest of ribs. Omit picot cast-off edge, and cast off in rib.

VERSION 3

PLAIN BLACK MOHAIR WAISTCOAT WITH BLACK AND WHITE PICOT BORDER

MATERIALS
Yarns
200(250 : 300)g/7(9 : 11)oz black mohair (A), 100(125 : 125)g/4(5 : 5)oz white cotton DK (C), 75g(3oz) black cotton 4-ply (D)
Needles and tension as for Version 1.

METHOD
Work the back and fronts as for Version 1 but in yarn A only in st st.
The making up and edgings are worked as for Version 1.

VERSION 2

JACKET WITHOUT DECORATION

This version is worked exactly as for Version 1 but using a plain-coloured yarn for B. Needles and tension remain the same.

METHOD

Omit all decoration and when working the sleeves work 2 rows of K1, P1 rib in A before beginning the main pattern.
As for Version 1 14 buttons are needed.
Add shirring elastic to back.

VERSION 3

JACKET KNITTED IN ONE YARN ONLY WITHOUT DECORATION

MATERIALS

Yarn
Use double-knit weight: 825(850 : 875)g/30(30 : 31)oz multi-coloured cotton slub (A)
Needles and tension as for Version 1.

BACK

(Worked in one piece)
With 4½mm needles and A, cast on 100(108 : 116)sts and work 2 rows in K1, P1 rib. Now starting with a K row, work straight in st st until back measures 19(21.5 : 24)cm/7½(8½ : 9½)in from cast-on edge, ending with a WS row.

Decrease for waist
Next row: K, and dec 34(36 : 38)sts evenly across row – 66(72 : 78)sts. Work 5 rows in st st.
Increase row: Inc 1 st in every 3rd st of row – 88(96 : 104)sts.
Cont straight in st st until back measures 48(51 : 54)cm/19(20 : 21)in from cast-on edge, ending with a WS row.

Shape armholes
Cast off 8 sts at beg of next 2 rows – 72(80 : 88)sts.
Dec 1 st at armhole edge at beg of every row until 66(74 : 82)sts remain.
Now cont straight until back measures 73(76 : 79)cm/28¾(30 : 31)in from cast-on edge, ending with a WS row.

Shape shoulders
Cast off 6(7 : 8)sts at beg of next 6 rows.
Cast off rem 30(32 : 34)sts for back neck.
Work the rest of the pieces as for Version 1 but all in one colour. On sleeves work 2 rows of K1, P1 rib as for Version 2.

Pocket tops
Work to ***, then cast off in rib.
Complete as for Version 1, but omit all decoration and shirring elastic.

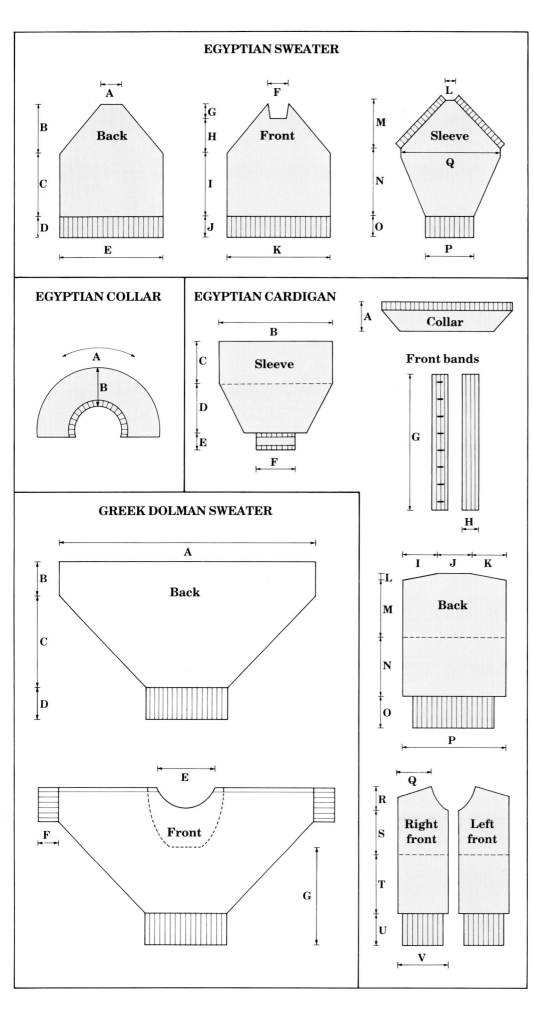

MEASUREMENTS

The diagrams indicate approximate shape of pattern pieces for each garment. Shaded areas indicate ribbed sections.

EGYPTIAN SWEATER (p 13)

A 10(11)cm/4(4¼)in
B 23(25)cm/9(9¾)in
C 30cm/11¾in
D 10cm/4in
E 50(55)cm/19¾(21¾)in
F 10(11)cm/4(4¼)in
G 7cm/2¾in
H 16(18)cm/6¼(7)in
I 30cm/11¾in
J 10cm/4in
K 50(55)cm/19¾(21¾)in
L 4(5)cm/1½(2)in
M 23(25)cm/9(9¾)in
N 32cm/12½in
O 10cm/4in
P 24(29)cm/9½(11½)in
Q 49(54)cm/19¼(21¼)in

EGYPTIAN COLLAR (p 19)

A 120cm/47¼in
B 20cm/7¾in

EGYPTIAN CARDIGAN (p 21)

A 14cm/5½in
B 55(59:63)cm/22¾(23¼:24¾)in
C 20cm/7¾in
D 23(25:28)cm/9(9¾:11)in
E 8cm/3¼in
F 20(21.5:23)cm/7¾(8½:9)in
G 64(67:69)cm/25¼(26½:27¼)in
H 3cm/1¼in
I 16.5(18.25:20)cm/6½(7:7¾)in
J 18cm/7in
K 16.5(18.25:20)cm/6½(7:7¾)in
L 3cm/1¼in
M 27cm/10½in
N 28(31:33)cm/11(12½:13)in
O 15cm/6in
P 51(54.5:58)cm/20(21½:22¾)in
Q 16.5(18.25:20)cm/6½(7:7¾)in
R 9cm/3½in
S 21cm/8¼in
T 28(31:33)cm/11(12½:13)in
U 15cm/6in
V 25(27:29)cm/9¾(10½:11½)in

GREEK DOLMAN SWEATER (p 30)

A 124(129:134)cm/48¾(50¾:52¾)in
B 16cm/6¼in
C 43cm/17in
D 15cm/6in
E 28cm/11in
F 10cm/4in
G 46cm/18in

MEASUREMENTS cont.

ROMAN SWEATER (p 36)

- **A** 9cm/3½in
- **B** 2cm/¾in
- **C** 25cm/9¾in
- **D** 35cm/13¾in
- **E** 13cm/5in
- **F** 52.5(55)cm/20¾(21¾)in
- **G** 39cm/15¼in
- **H** 21cm/8¼in
- **I** 10cm/4in
- **J** 17cm/6¾in
- **K** 35cm/13¾in
- **L** 13cm/5in
- **M** 52.5(55)cm/20¾in(21¾)in
- **N** 12(13)cm/4¾(5)in
- **O** 12cm/4¾in
- **P** 36cm/14¼in
- **Q** 5cm/2in
- **R** 30(34)cm/11¾(13½)in
- **S** 49(52)cm/19¼(20½)in

BYZANTINE SWEATER (p 48)

- **A** 50cm/19¾in
- **B** 37(39:41)/14½(15¼:16¼)in
- **C** 9cm/3½in
- **D** 19cm/7½in
- **E** 9cm/3½in
- **F** 30cm/11¾in
- **G** 32cm/12½in
- **H** 51(54:57)cm/20(21¼:22½)in
- **I** 69cm/27¼in
- **J** 16(17.5:19)cm/6¼(7:7½)in
- **K** 31cm/12¼in
- **L** 38cm/15in
- **M** 51(54:57)cm/20(21¼:22½)in

MEDIEVAL SWEATER (p 58)

- **A** 13(15:17)cm/5(6:6¾)in
- **B** 11cm/4¼in
- **C** 17cm/6¾in
- **D** 33(35:38)cm/13(13¾:15)in
- **E** 11cm/4¼in
- **F** 52.5(56:60)cm/20¾(22:23½)in
- **G** 70cm/27½in
- **H** 40cm/15¾in
- **I** 11cm/4¼in
- **J** 40cm/15¾in

RENAISSANCE SWEATER I (p64)

- **A** 10.5(12)cm/4½(4¾)in
- **B** 3cm/1¼in
- **C** 25cm/9¾in
- **D** 15cm/6in
- **E** 5cm/2in
- **F** 15cm/6in
- **G** 52(54)cm/20½(21¼)in
- **H** 40(42)cm/15¾(16½)in
- **I** 18(19)cm/7(7½)in
- **J** 12cm/4¾in
- **K** 16cm/6¼in
- **L** 15cm/6in
- **M** 5cm/2in
- **N** 15cm/6in
- **O** 52(54)cm/20½(21¼)in
- **P** 20cm/7¾in
- **Q** 25cm/9¾in
- **R** 33cm/13in
- **S** 7cm/2¾in
- **T** 40cm/15¾in
- **U** 46cm/18in
- **V** 20cm/7¾in **W** 60cm/23½in

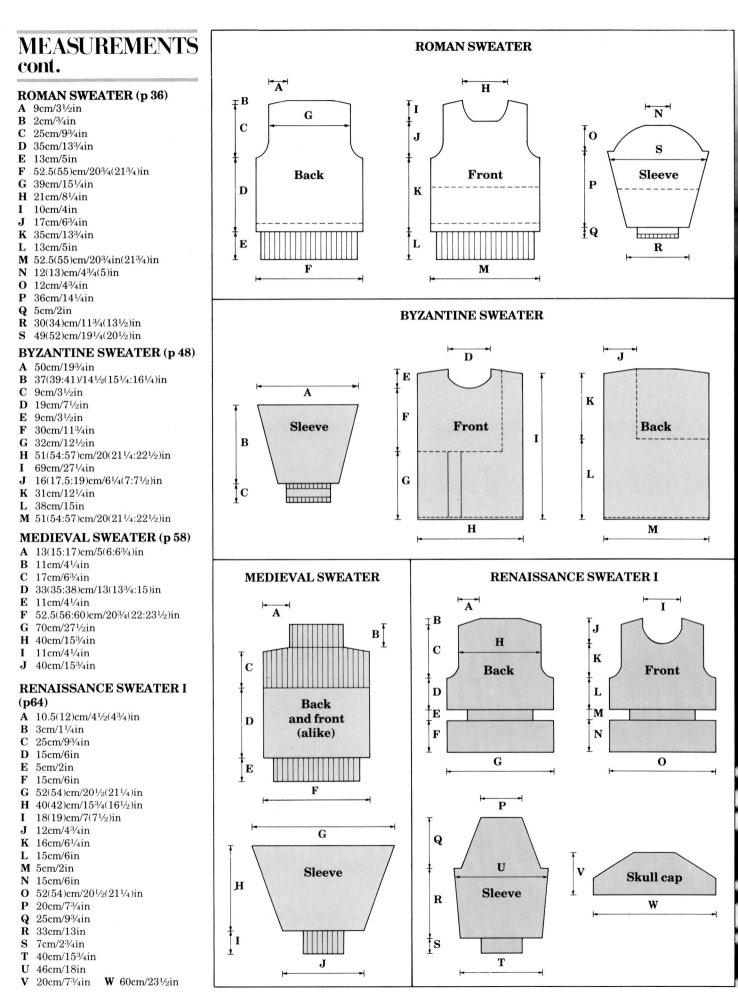

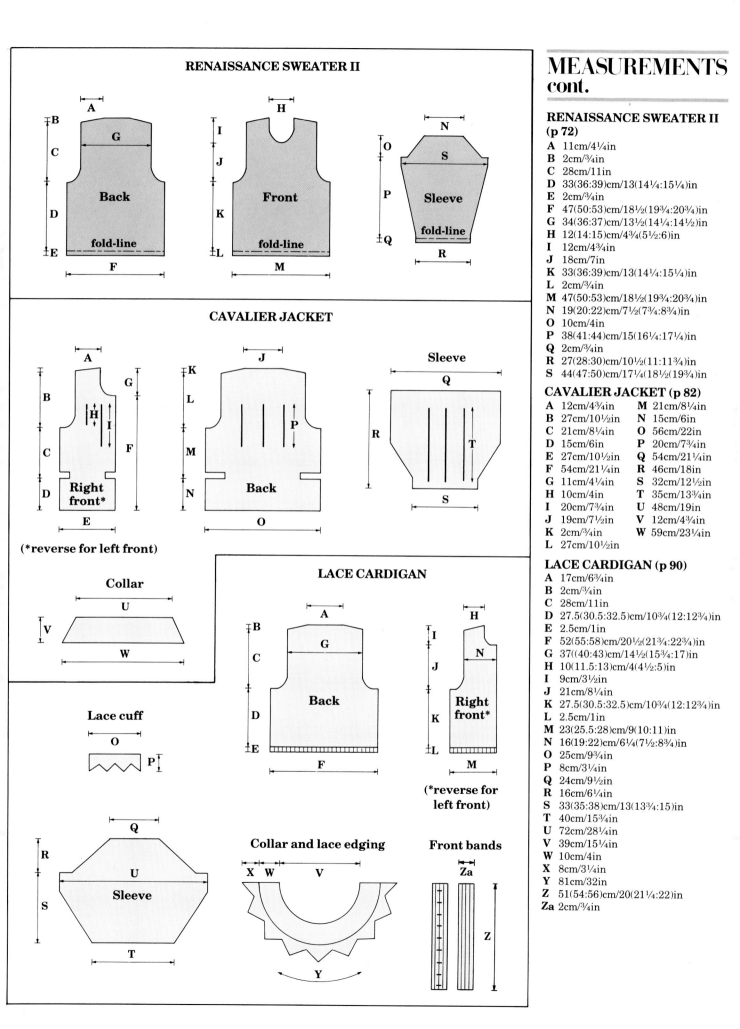

RENAISSANCE SWEATER II

Back fold-line

Front fold-line

Sleeve fold-line

CAVALIER JACKET

Right front* (*reverse for left front)

Back

Sleeve

Collar

LACE CARDIGAN

Lace cuff

Back

Right front* (*reverse for left front)

Sleeve

Collar and lace edging

Front bands

MEASUREMENTS cont.

RENAISSANCE SWEATER II (p 72)

A 11cm/4¼in
B 2cm/¾in
C 28cm/11in
D 33(36:39)cm/13(14¼:15¼)in
E 2cm/¾in
F 47(50:53)cm/18½(19¾:20¾)in
G 34(36:37)cm/13½(14¼:14½)in
H 12(14:15)cm/4¾(5½:6)in
I 12cm/4¾in
J 18cm/7in
K 33(36:39)cm/13(14¼:15¼)in
L 2cm/¾in
M 47(50:53)cm/18½(19¾:20¾)in
N 19(20:22)cm/7½(7¾:8¾)in
O 10cm/4in
P 38(41:44)cm/15(16¼:17¼)in
Q 2cm/¾in
R 27(28:30)cm/10½(11:11¾)in
S 44(47:50)cm/17¼(18½:19¾)in

CAVALIER JACKET (p 82)

A 12cm/4¾in   **M** 21cm/8¼in
B 27cm/10½in   **N** 15cm/6in
C 21cm/8¼in   **O** 56cm/22in
D 15cm/6in   **P** 20cm/7¾in
E 27cm/10½in   **Q** 54cm/21¼in
F 54cm/21¼in   **R** 46cm/18in
G 11cm/4¼in   **S** 32cm/12½in
H 10cm/4in   **T** 35cm/13¾in
I 20cm/7¾in   **U** 48cm/19in
J 19cm/7½in   **V** 12cm/4¾in
K 2cm/¾in   **W** 59cm/23¼in
L 27cm/10½in

LACE CARDIGAN (p 90)

A 17cm/6¾in
B 2cm/¾in
C 28cm/11in
D 27.5(30.5:32.5)cm/10¾(12:12¾)in
E 2.5cm/1in
F 52(55:58)cm/20½(21¾:22¾)in
G 37((40:43)cm/14½(15¾:17)in
H 10(11.5:13)cm/4(4½:5)in
I 9cm/3½in
J 21cm/8¼in
K 27.5(30.5:32.5)cm/10¾(12:12¾)in
L 2.5cm/1in
M 23(25.5:28)cm/9(10:11)in
N 16(19:22)cm/6¼(7½:8¾)in
O 25cm/9¾in
P 8cm/3¼in
Q 24cm/9½in
R 16cm/6¼in
S 33(35:38)cm/13(13¾:15)in
T 40cm/15¾in
U 72cm/28¼in
V 39cm/15¼in
W 10cm/4in
X 8cm/3¼in
Y 81cm/32in
Z 51(54:56)cm/20(21¼:22)in
Za 2cm/¾in

MEASUREMENTS cont.

BROCADE WAISTCOAT (p 96)

A 19cm/7½in
B 2cm/¾in
C 29cm/11½in
D 20cm/7¾in
E 52(55:59)cm/20½(21¾:23¼)in
F 39(42:45)cm/15¼(16½:17¾)in
G 10(11.5:13)cm/4(4½:5)in
H 6cm/2¼in
I 25cm/9¾in
J 20cm/7¾in
K 23(25:27)cm/9(9¾:10½)in

18TH CENTURY JACKET (p 102)

A 31cm/12¼in
B 8cm/3¼in
C 38(41:44)cm/15(16¼:17¼)in
D 31cm/12¼in
E 50cm/19¾in
F 8(8.5:9)cm/3¼(3½:3½)in
G 1.5cm/¾in
H 25cm/9¾in
I 28(28.5:29)cm/11(11¼:11½)in
J 19(21.5:24)cm/7½(8½:9½)in
K 1cm/½in
L 28(30:32)cm/11(11¾:12½)in
M 24(26.5:29)cm/9½(10½:11½)in
N 10(11.5:13)cm/4(4½:5)in
O 8.5cm/3¼in
P 18cm/7in
Q 30(33:36)cm/11¾(13:14¼)in
R 17cm/6¾in
S 1cm/½in
T 28(30:32)cm/11(11¾:12½)in
U 24(26.5:29)cm/9½(10½:11½)cm
V 12cm/4¾in
W 13cm/5in

18TH-CENTURY WAISTCOAT (p 109)

A 14cm/5½in
B 2cm/¾in
C 26cm/10¼in
D 28(31:34)cm/11(12¼:13½)in
E 2cm/¾in
F 45(48:51)cm/17¾(19:20)in
G 10(11:12)cm/4(4¼:4¾)in
H 38cm/15in
I 18(21:24)cm/7(8¼:9½)in
J 2cm/¾in
K 23(24.5:25.5)cm/9(9¾:10)in

18TH-CENTURY SWEATER (p 112)

A 17cm/6¾in
B 2cm/¾in
C 25cm/9¾in
D 27cm/10½in
E 7cm/2¾in
F 47.5(50:53)cm/18¾(19¾:20¾)in
G 10(11:12)cm/4(4¼:4¾)in
H 15cm/6in
I 12cm/4¾in
J 27cm/10½in
K 7cm/2¾in
L 47.5(50:53)cm/18¾(19¾:20¾)in
M 25cm/9¾in
N 12cm/4¾in
O 25.5cm/10in   **Q** 40cm/15¾in
P 2.5cm/1in   **R** 59cm/23¼

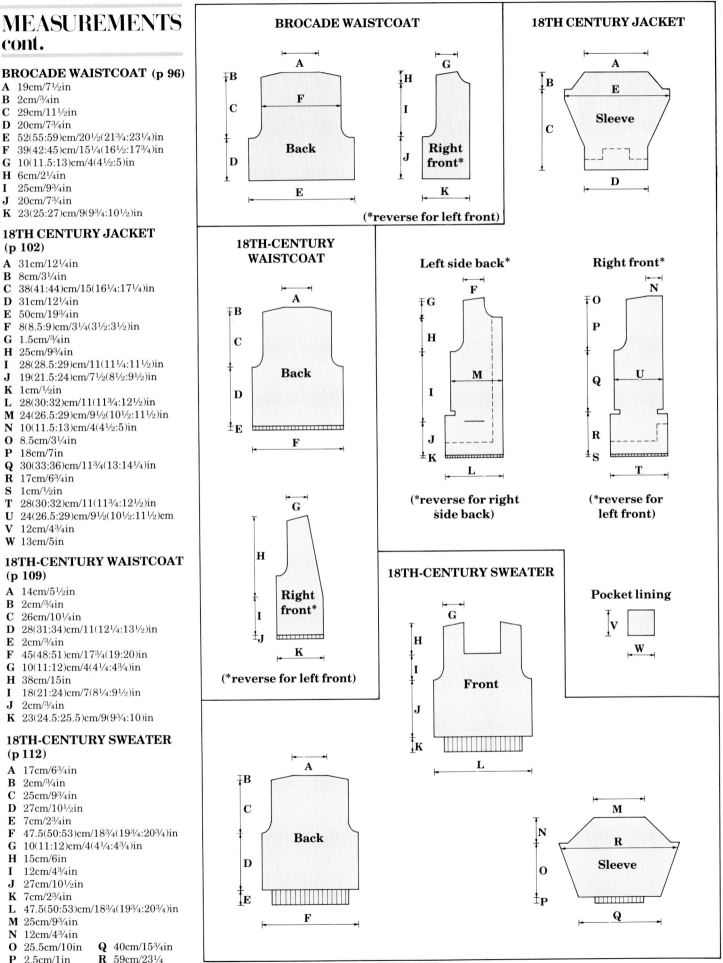

BROCADE WAISTCOAT

Back

Right front*

(*reverse for left front)

18TH CENTURY JACKET

Sleeve

18TH-CENTURY WAISTCOAT

Back

Right front*

(*reverse for left front)

Left side back*

(*reverse for right side back)

Right front*

(*reverse for left front)

18TH-CENTURY SWEATER

Front

Back

Sleeve

Pocket lining

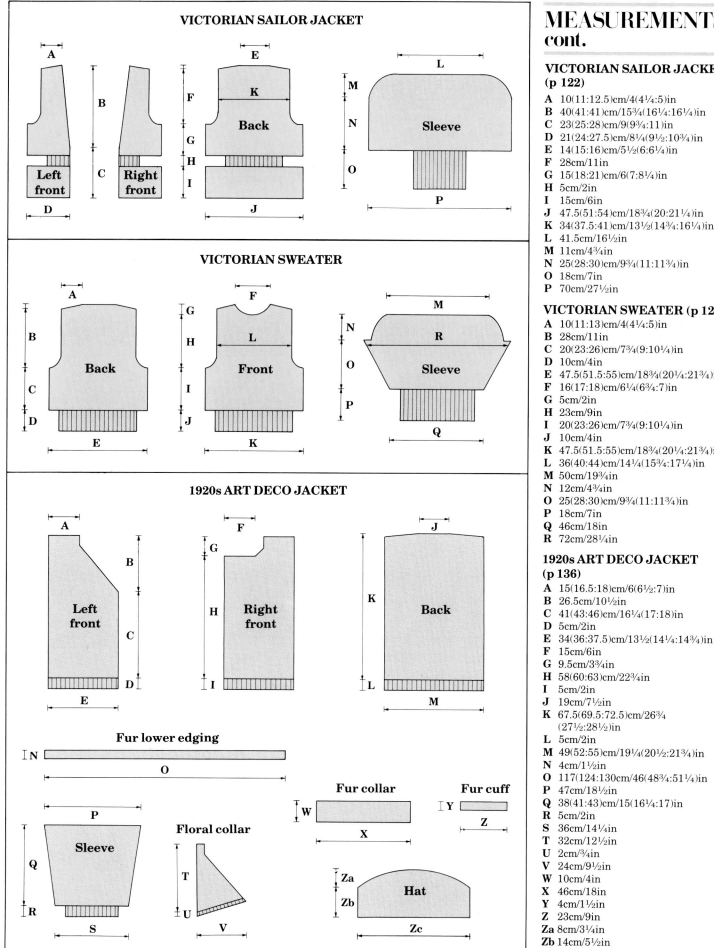

VICTORIAN SAILOR JACKET

VICTORIAN SWEATER

1920s ART DECO JACKET

Fur lower edging

Fur collar

Fur cuff

Floral collar

Hat

VICTORIAN SAILOR JACKET (p 122)

A 10(11:12.5)cm/4(4¼:5)in
B 40(41:41)cm/15¾(16¼:16¼)in
C 23(25:28)cm/9(9¾:11)in
D 21(24:27.5)cm/8¼(9½:10¾)in
E 14(15:16)cm/5½(6:6¼)in
F 28cm/11in
G 15(18:21)cm/6(7:8¼)in
H 5cm/2in
I 15cm/6in
J 47.5(51:54)cm/18¾(20:21¼)in
K 34(37.5:41)cm/13½(14¾:16¼)in
L 41.5cm/16½in
M 11cm/4¾in
N 25(28:30)cm/9¾(11:11¾)in
O 18cm/7in
P 70cm/27½in

VICTORIAN SWEATER (p 129)

A 10(11:13)cm/4(4¼:5)in
B 28cm/11in
C 20(23:26)cm/7¾(9:10¼)in
D 10cm/4in
E 47.5(51.5:55)cm/18¾(20¼:21¾)in
F 16(17:18)cm/6¼(6¾:7)in
G 5cm/2in
H 23cm/9in
I 20(23:26)cm/7¾(9:10¼)in
J 10cm/4in
K 47.5(51.5:55)cm/18¾(20¼:21¾)in
L 36(40:44)cm/14¼(15¾:17¼)in
M 50cm/19¾in
N 12cm/4¾in
O 25(28:30)cm/9¾(11:11¾)in
P 18cm/7in
Q 46cm/18in
R 72cm/28¼in

1920s ART DECO JACKET (p 136)

A 15(16.5:18)cm/6(6½:7)in
B 26.5cm/10½in
C 41(43:46)cm/16¼(17:18)in
D 5cm/2in
E 34(36:37.5)cm/13½(14¼:14¾)in
F 15cm/6in
G 9.5cm/3¾in
H 58(60:63)cm/22¾in
I 5cm/2in
J 19cm/7½in
K 67.5(69.5:72.5)cm/26¾ (27½:28½)in
L 5cm/2in
M 49(52:55)cm/19¼(20½:21¾)in
N 4cm/1½in
O 117(124:130cm/46(48¾:51¼)in
P 47cm/18½in
Q 38(41:43)cm/15(16¼:17)in
R 5cm/2in
S 36cm/14¼in
T 32cm/12½in
U 2cm/¾in
V 24cm/9½in
W 10cm/4in
X 46cm/18in
Y 4cm/1½in
Z 23cm/9in
Za 8cm/3¼in
Zb 14cm/5½in
Zc 55.5cm/21¾in

MEASUREMENTS cont.

1920s CABLE SWEATER (p 143)

A 11.5(13:14)cm/4½(5:5½)in
B 59(61:64)cm/23¼(24:25¼)in
C 5cm/2in
D 48(51:53.5)cm/19(20:21)in
E 25cm/9¾in
F 16cm/6¼in
G 43(45:48)cm/17(17¾:19)in
H 5cm/2in
I 48(51:53.5)cm/19(20:21)in
J 50cm/19¾in
K 42cm/16½in
L 5cm/2in
M 33cm/13in

RAGLAN JACKET (p 150)

A 88cm/34¾in)
B 20.5(22.5)cm/8(9)in
C 12cm/4¾in
D 31.5(33.5)cm/12½(13¼)in
E 39cm/15¼in
F 5cm/2in
G 12(13)cm/4¾(5)in
H 31.5(33.5)cm/12½(13¼)in
I 39cm/15¼in
J 5cm/2in
K 46cm/18in)
L 6.5cm/2½in
M 31.5(33.5)cm/12½(13¼)in
N 28cm/11in
O 5cm/2in
P 32(36)cm/12½(14¼)in
Q 3cm/1¼in
R 60(64)cm/23½(25¼)in

RIBBED SKIRT (p 157)

A 8cm/3¼
B 91cm/35¾in
C 75(86:96)cm/29½(33¼:37¾)in

FAIR ISLE SWEATER (p 158)

A 14(16:17)cm/5½(6¼:6¾)in
B 53(56:58)cm/20¾(22:22¾)in
C 13cm/5in
D 45(49.5:54)cm/17¾(19½:21¼)in
E 16(18:19)cm/6¼(7:7½)in
F 28cm/11in
G 25(28:30)cm/9¾(11:11¾)in
H 13cm/5in
I 45(49.5:54)cm/17¾(19½:21¼)in
J 16(18:19)cm/6¼(7:7½)in
K 8cm/3¼in
L 45(48:50)cm/17¾(19:19¾)in
M 13cm/5in
N 45(49.5:54)cm/17¾(19½:21¼)in
O 49cm/19¼in
P 35(38:40)cm/13¾(15:15¾)in
Q 8cm/3¼in
R 35.5cm/14in

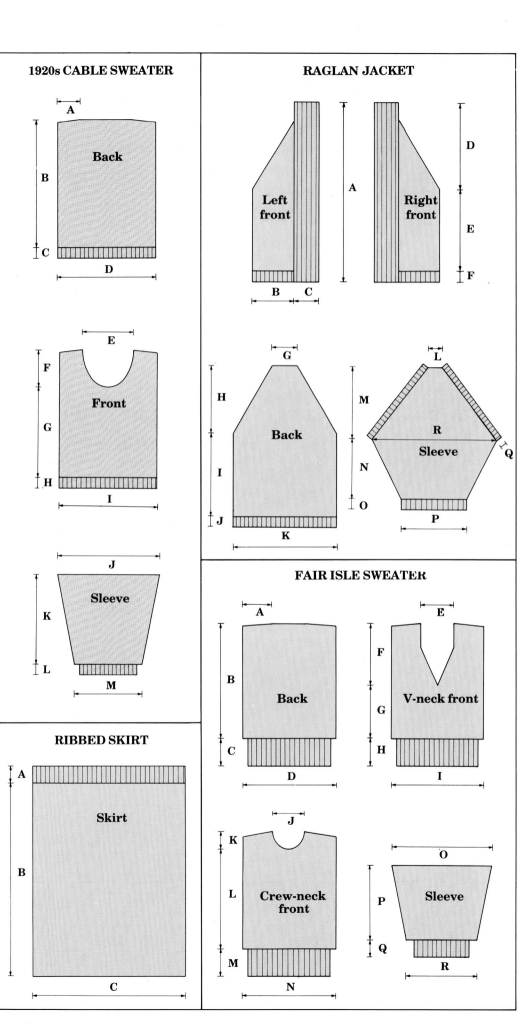

1920s CABLE SWEATER — Back, Front, Sleeve

RAGLAN JACKET — Left front, Right front, Back, Sleeve

RIBBED SKIRT — Skirt

FAIR ISLE SWEATER — Back, V-neck front, Crew-neck front, Sleeve

NOTES AND ABBREVIATIONS

YARN AMOUNTS

Because we do not specify a particular make of yarn for each garment, and because of the wide variety of yarns used together in some of the garments in this book, it is difficult to give exact quantities of yarn needed. (The yarn amounts given for Versions 2 and 3 of each garment are approximate, as these versions have not actually been knitted and quantities have been calculated from Version 1.)

It is always wise to buy more yarn than you may need rather than run out and be unable to buy more of the same dye lot. You may have small amounts of yarn left over but these can always be used on future garments, so this is no problem for the keen knitter.

TENSION

It is *very* important to check your tension. You must match your tension to that stated in each pattern by knitting a square in the correct yarns before actually starting to knit the garment. The number of stitches and rows to the cm (in) must be the same as those given in the pattern. If not, the garment will end up too small or too large.

CLEANING

Read the ball bands for general instructions on washing, etc. Never wash any knitted fabric in hot water as this can result in shrinkage and matting. If the ball advises hand-washing then do so in lukewarm water and use a mild liquid detergent (shampoo is always good). Never lift the wet garment up out of the water as this will result in stretching; always support the weight with both hands and squeeze out excess moisture gently – do not wring. The drying process may be speeded up by spin-drying, but this is not advisable for garments with beads or delicate trimmings. The damp garment may be put inside a pillow-case (loosely closed with safety-pins or a few tacking stitches to keep the garment inside) to prevent it from stretching out of shape whilst spinning. It can then be given a short spin, carefully pulled back into shape and laid out flat to dry.

If there are many different types of yarn in the same garment, or if it is embroidered or beaded, then I would advise dry-cleaning. It may be necessary to remove the more elaborate trimmings unless you can find a specialist cleaner who can deal with these. You can give your original tension swatch (which can even be trimmed as specified) to the dry cleaner to test for suitability.

CARE OF GARMENT

It is worth taking a little time and trouble to look after your sweater. For example, if it is one of the decorated garments, buy a few extra beads and trimmings so that you can replace and repair them in years to come. Some yarns are prone to pilling (forming bobbles); if so, these can be removed by hand or with Sellotape. Mohair sweaters can be brushed with a teasel or hairbrush to keep them soft and fluffy.

PATTERN NOTES

● Every pattern is graded with one to four symbols denoting the standard of knitting required, as follows:

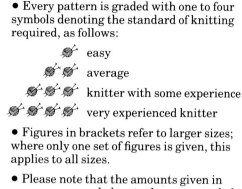

● Figures in brackets refer to larger sizes; where only one set of figures is given, this applies to all sizes.

● Please note that the amounts given in ounces are rounded up to the nearest whole ounce (1 ounce = 28.35 grams).

● When working from charts, read knit rows from right to left and purl rows from left to right unless otherwise stated.

NOTES FOR AMERICAN KNITTERS

● Both metric and imperial measurements are used throughout the book; American needle sizes are also given, so the patterns should be easily followed by American knitters. However, there are a few differences in knitting terminology and yarn names which are given below.

Knitting terminology

UK	US
cast off	bind off
stocking stitch	stockinette stitch
tension	gauge
work straight	work even

Yarns

UK	US
Aran	fisherman/medium weight
chunky	bulky
double knitting	knitting worsted
4-ply	lightweight

ABBREVIATIONS

alt	alternate
approx	approximately
beg	beginning
cm	centimetres
cont	continue
dec	decrease
foll	following
g	grams
g st	garter stitch
in	inches
inc	increase
K	knit
LH	left hand
mm	millimetres
oz	ounces
P	purl
patt	pattern
psso	pass slipped st over
rem	remaining
rep	repeat
RH	right hand
RS	right side
sl	slip
st(s)	stitch(es)
st st	stocking stitch
tbl	through back of loops
tog	together
WS	wrong side
yf	yarn forward
yon	yarn over needle

KNITTING NEEDLE CONVERSION TABLE

Metric	US	Old UK	Metric	US	Old UK
2mm	0	14	5mm	8	6
2¼mm	1	13	5½mm	9	5
2½mm			6mm	10	4
2¾mm	2	12	6½mm	10½	3
3mm		11	7mm		2
3¼mm	3	10	7½mm		1
3½mm	4		8mm	11	0
3¾mm	5	9	9mm	13	00
4mm	6	8	10mm	15	000
4½mm	7	7			

LIST OF SUPPLIERS

The firms listed below supply the actual yarns used for the garments in this book. Addresses for suppliers' agents outside the UK and USA have also been given. However, because no particular brand of yarn is specified in the patterns, knitters have complete freedom of choice: any brand of yarn can be used providing it corresponds with the weight specified in the relevant pattern; texture can also change, i.e. a sweater knitted in DK cotton can equally well be knitted in DK wool.

YARNS USED IN THIS BOOK

For fancy yarns as seen in:
30s & 40s Raglan Jacket

COLOURTWIST LTD
10 Mayfield Avenue Ind. Park
Weyhill
Andover
Hants SP11 8HU
Tel: (026 477) 3369

For silk yarns as seen in:
Renaissance Sweater II
Cavalier Lace Cardigan
18th-Century Waistcoat
18th-Century Sweater

NATURALLY BEAUTIFUL LTD
Main Street
Dent
Cumbria LA10 5QL
Tel: (05875) 421

For double-knit wool/cotton, chunky tweed yarns and cotton chenille as seen in:
Egyptian Sweater and Cardigan
Roman Sweater
Cavalier Jacket
18th-Century Sweater
Victorian Sweater
30s & 40s Fair Isle Sweater

ROWAN YARNS
Green Lane Mill
Holmfirth
West Yorkshire HD7 1RW
Tel: (0484) 681881

Agents:
CREATIVE FASHION CENTRE
PO Box 45 083
Epuni Railway
Lower Hutt
New Zealand

ESTELLE DESIGNS AND SALES LTD
38 Continental Place
Scarborough
Ontario
Canada M1R 2TA
Tel: (416) 2989922

SUNSPUN ENTERPRISES PTY LTD
195 Canterbury Road
Canterbury 3126
Australia
Tel: 03 830 1609

JUMPERS
Admiral's Court
31 Tyrwhitt Avenue
Rosebank 2196
Johannesburg
South Africa
Tel: (011) 788 3798

For viscose and fancy yarns (Noro) as seen in:
Egyptian Cardigan
Greek Dolman Sweater
18th-Century Jacket
1920s Cable Sweater

TEXERE YARNS
College Mill
Barkerend Road
Bradford BD3 9AQ
Tel: (0274) 22191

Viscose spinners:
LEIDSCHE WOLSPINNERIJ, NV
3901 Es Veenendaal
Stationsplein 6
Netherlands

For lurex yarns as seen in:
Egyptian Cardigan
Roman Sweater
Byzantine & Medieval Sweaters
Renaissance (both sweaters)

TEXERE YARNS
College Mill
Barkerend Road
Bradford BD3 9AQ
Tel: (0274) 22191

For mohair, Aran and angora yarns as seen in:
Medieval & Byzantine Sweaters
Renaissance Sweater I
Victorian Sailor Jacket
1920s Art Deco Jacket
30s & 40s Raglan Jacket

PAMELA WISE
101–105 Goswell Road
London EC1V 7ER
Tel: (071) 490 0037

Agent:
SOUTHERN CROSS YARNS LTD
49 Spadina Avenue
Toronto
Canada M5V 2J1
Tel: (416) 593 8988

UK RETAIL OUTLETS

COLOURWAY
112a Westbourne Grove
London W2 5RU
Tel: (071) 229 1432

CREATIVITY
45 New Oxford Street
London WC1
Tel: (071) 240 2945

RIES WOOLS
242 High Holborn
London WC1V 7DZ
Tel: (071) 242 7721

SHEPHERDS PURSE
2 John Street
Bath BA1 2JL
Tel: (0225) 310790

BEADS, FEATHERS, STONES ETC

ELLS AND FARRIER LTD
The Bead House
5 Princes Street
Hanover Square
London W1R 8PH
Tel: (071) 629 9964/5

(good catalogue)

INTERESTING BUTTONS

THE BUTTON BOX
44 Bedford Street
Covent Garden
London WC2E 9HA
Tel: (071) 2716/2841

(send SAE for catalogue)

JESSIE'S BUTTON BOX
Great Western Antiques Centre
Bartlett Street
Bath
Tel: (0225) 20686

(common number for stall holders)

USA YARN SUPPLIERS

MERINO WOOL COMPANY
230 Fifth Avenue
New York, NY 10001
Tel: (212) 686 0050

NORO YARNS
Agent:
Mr Sion Elaluf
Knitting Fever
180 Babylon Turnpike
New York, NY 11575
Tel: (516) 546 3600
(800) 645 3457

**ROWAN YARNS
(USA & CANADA)**
Agent:
Westminster Trading
6 Northern Boulevard
Amherst
New Hampshire 03031
Tel: (0603) 886 5041

USA RETAIL OUTLETS

SUSAN BATES INC
1818 Industrial Way
Redwood City
Calif 94603
Tel: (800) 243 0810

ANNY BLATT YARNS
Applegate Square
29775 N. Western Highway
Southfield
Mich 48034
Tel: (313) 354 2470

FIBER WORKS
313 East 45th Street
New York, NY 10017
Tel: (212) 286 9116

SCHOOL PRODUCTS CO INC
1201 Broadway
New York, NY 10001
Tel: (212) 679 3516

SOFT SPECTRUM
216 Grand Avenue
Pacific Grove
Calif 93950
Tel: (408) 373 8210

'STRAW INTO GOLD'
3006 San Pablo Avenue
Berkeley
Calif 94702
Tel: (415) 548 5241

TENDER BUTTONS
143 East 62nd Street
New York
NY 10021
Tel: (212) 758 7004

WILDE YARNS
3705 Main Street
Dept Y
Philadelphia
PA 19127
Tel: (215) 482 8800